SICILIAN
STUDIES

Also by Jacqueline Alio and Louis Mendola

The Peoples of Sicily
A Multicultural Legacy

Norman-Arab-Byzantine
Palermo, Monreale and Cefalù

Jacqueline Alio

Margaret, Queen of Sicily

Queens of Sicily 1061-1266

The Ferraris Chronicle
Popes, Emperors, and Deeds in Apulia 1096-1228

Women of Sicily
Saints, Queens and Rebels

Sicilian Food and Wine
The Cognoscente's Guide

Louis Mendola

The Kingdom of Sicily 1130-1860

Sicilian Genealogy and Heraldry

Sicily's Rebellion against King Charles
The Story of the Sicilian Vespers

Frederick, Conrad and Manfred of Hohenstaufen, Kings of Sicily
The Chronicle of Nicholas of Jamsilla

Manfred of Hohenstaufen, King of Sicily

The Battle of Benevento according to
Andrew of Hungary and Saba Malaspina

SICILIAN STUDIES

A Guide and Syllabus for Educators

Jacqueline Alio
Louis Mendola

Published by Trinacria Editions, New York.

Legal Deposit: Library of Congress, British Library (and Bodleian Libraries, Cambridge University Library, Trinity College Library, National Libraries of Scotland and Wales), Italian National Libraries (Rome, Florence), Sicilian Regional Library (Palermo).

Some material in this volume appeared in earlier books by Jacqueline Alio and Louis Mendola, and is used by permission.

All translations contained herein are by the authors. Illustrations, photographs, image editing, maps and cover design by Louis Mendola. The title of this book was assigned a Library of Congress Control Number on 24 January 2018. CIP was registered by the British Library through Bibliographic Data Services on 31 January 2018.

ORCID identifier Calogera Jacqueline Alio: 0000-0003-1134-1217
ORCID identifier Louis André Mendola: 0000-0002-1965-6072

Printed in the United States of America on acid-free paper.

ISBN 9781943639182 (print)
ISBN 9781943639199 (ebook)

Library of Congress Control Number 2018901042

A CIP catalogue record for this book is available from the British Library.

To Carlo and Camilla
de Bourbon of the Two Sicilies
Duke and Duchess of Castro

Roger II depicted as a Byzantine basileus crowned by Christ in engraving based on mosaic in Martorana church, Palermo

PREFACE

About a year after the publication of *The Peoples of Sicily: A Multicultural Legacy* we learned, quite unexpectedly, that university professors in anglophone countries were using our book to teach courses with a focus on cultural diversity, or even ancient and medieval Sicilian history generally. For the most part, these were undergraduate courses or seminars, and in one case a summer course on historical Mediterranean multiculturalism held in Sicily, and they did not always fall within the purview of departments that oversee Italian cultural and linguistic studies. By 2018, several American high schools were using the book, and thousands of copies had been sold.

Increasingly, we were asked to give lectures on the multicultural history of the world's most conquered island. Professors and travel agents solicited our advice on how to plan study tours of Sicily based on *The Peoples of Sicily* and our other books.

Until just a few years ago, there was not enough material available (and in print) in English to teach a course having a focus on our island. Indeed, there were not even many books dedicated to Sicilian tourism or Sicilian wines. Digital downloads and print-on-demand books, including reprints of important works published over a century ago, are a recent development.

Long before the publication of our own books, we were frequently asked to recommend informative works. Some books, while interesting and perhaps useful in certain respects, had obvious flaws. A book written by an American on the island's culinary traditions referred to rural Sicilians its author met as "peasants," while a book written by a Briton on Sicilian history expressed the eccentric notion that there is no organized crime in Sicily. Such perspectives made it difficult to recommend certain books without serious caveats on our part.

Very few of the Siculophile academicians who contacted us had ancestral ties to Italy. Indeed, a professor in the United States informed us that she encountered scornful opposition from a self-interested, Italian-born academic in her department "offended" that any Italian medieval literature having roots beyond Tuscany would be studied at all!

Truth is the simplest paradigm of all, yet the most difficult to achieve.

Informative, unbiased books are available in English. Many reflect current historiography and research.

This volume's only social or intellectual "agenda" is to indicate and describe accurate, useful strategies and resources that will permit you, the instructor, to formulate a course, lecture or seminar that presents Sicilian history, literature or culture to students who are not proficient in Italian.

But it's not just for educators. Anybody seeking a reliable outline will benefit from these candid recommendations.

This book was written because it needed to be written, and because there is now just enough material available in English to teach something in this language about our favorite island. We wish you and your students a pleasant voyage of discovery, and we hope that your travels take you to Sicily.

ACKNOWLEDGMENTS

The authors would like to thank their many readers and colleagues for the comments and suggestions that led to this book being written. Its publication was much belated, and the delay merits explanation.

This volume was first contemplated some years ago. At that time, however, there was a dearth of books in print to permit the formulation of anything like a syllabus or canon for a course of study.

Not only was that true in English but, paradoxically, in Italian. Except for papers read by a handful of scholars, the study of Sicily was generally discouraged in the erstwhile Kingdom of Italy from 1860 until 1945 because a major biography of, for example, a medieval leader like Roger II or Frederick II might remind Sicilians of an identity suppressed by the proponents of Italian nationalism.

When it wasn't being disparaged through an effort of the victors to vilify the vanquished, the House of Bourbon, which ruled Sicily until unification, was simply ignored, effectively erased from the pages of history.

This censorship finally ended with the liberation of our island by Allied forces in 1943, but by then the field was bereft of major works dedicated to Sicily. As the Italian professoriate was full of men educated during the Fascist era (Italian women could not even vote until 1945), no such works were immediately forthcoming.

Despite the new-found freedom of expression, decades would pass before Italians began to write much about the Sicilian kingdom that had flourished into the nineteenth century. The first international Italian conference on the Normans of Sicily was held in Palermo only in 1972, and only one paper was presented by a woman.

To fill the void were Italian translations of books by foreign scholars such as Moses Finley, Denis Mack Smith, Steven Runciman, Harold Acton, John Julius Norwich and Lynn Townsend White. Today the chief biographies available in Italian on the thirteenth-century ruler Frederick II are translations of the books by David Abulafia and Ernst Kantorowicz.

Hardly anybody in Italy spoke English before 1980 or even 2000. The Fascist regime had banned the teaching of that language, and it took generations to train enough English teachers to staff Italian schools. This deficiency was aggravated by the egregious failure of the Italian state to recognize the global importance of English over French. Consequently, few of Italy's professors can communicate very well in English.

Despite attracting increasing attention from foreign tourists and international scholars, Sicily's history and culture are still largely ignored by most Italians. While the merits of Dante and Boccaccio are undeniable, scarcely anybody knows that Sicilian, not Tuscan, was the first language to be identified with vernacular Italian literature, or even that paper was made in Sicily long before it was produced elsewhere in what is now Italy.

Every author who has written one of the books mentioned in this volume deserves recognition.

With one exception, the few images in this book that are not our work are in the public domain. Special thanks to the Metropolitan Museum of Art (New York) for permission to reproduce a photograph of the reliquary depicting Queen Margaret and Thomas Becket, licensed through the OASC (Open Access for Scholarly Content) program under accession number 63.160. This photograph is far superior to those we took at The Cloisters in Manhattan a few years ago.

We thank our friends at the *Best of Sicily Travel Guide,* which has been online for almost twenty years, and Sicily Concierge, a travel service, for their advice on the practicalities of travel outlined in Chapter 12.

– Jacqueline Alio and Louis Mendola

Palermo, March 2018

CONTENTS

INTRODUCTION

Like many places identified with a people and its culture, Sicily was once a nation. In its final incarnation, the kingdom that gave birth to an identity and several languages, Sicilian and Neapolitan prominent among them, was coterminous to *Magna Graecia,* the Greeks' *Megara Hellas.* Essentially, this was Sicily and most of the Apennine Peninsula south of Rome. Ruled by the House of Bourbon since 1734, that nation came to an end with the unification of Italy in 1860.

If the pre-unitary Italian states shown in one of this book's maps still existed, the idea of "Sicilian Studies," along with "Neapolitan Studies," would not elicit any more surprise than, for example, "Albanian Studies" or "Armenian Studies." One posits that even if "Italian Studies" existed in an "Italy" consisting of a federation of states, it might be divided into subfields, each with a focus on a different region: Piedmont, Tuscany, Campania, Lazio, Sicily, Sardinia, and so forth.

Casting a glance further back in time, had an earlier Sicilian dynasty, the Hohenstaufens, not been deposed in the thirteenth century, it is quite possible that Sicilian, not Tuscan, would have become the peninsula's vernacular language, for these emperor-kings ruled most of what is now Italy.

Leaving such speculation aside, the fact remains that Sicily, like Scotland, Aragon and many other parts of Europe, was once a sovereign kingdom with its own language, culture and laws.

Sicily's Greek tyrants and Arab emirs repose in memory, but some things inherited from the past survive. The Byzantine mosaics that cover the walls of the cathedral of Monreale Abbey, outside Palermo, are the largest display of that medieval art in Italy. Only in the former *Magna Graecia* will Italy's standing Greek temples be found. Palermo's splendid Palatine Chapel, with its ceiling of painted *muqarnas,* is unique in what was once the Fatimid Empire. Sicily boasts Italy's two oldest mikvehs. The Bourbons' royal palace at Caserta, outside Naples, is the largest edifice of its kind in Italy. Until recently, these treasures were regarded as well-kept secrets.

Charles III, the King of Naples and Sicily who ordered construction of the magnificent palace at Caserta, later sponsored the building of Saint Peter's, the first Roman Catholic church in New York; he was one of the greatest European monarchs of his time. (Today his direct descendant and namesake, to whom this book is dedicated, oversees a foundation that undertakes charitable works throughout Italy and abroad.)

Millions of families trace their roots to Sicily. They were Sicilian long before they were Italian. Theirs is a heritage of trimillennial continuity over countless generations.

Hence we encounter a fundamental flaw in the way that topics involving Sicily are often presented and taught. Rather than viewing "Sicilian Studies" as a sub-field of "Italian Studies," educators should consider it part of the broader fields of "Mediterranean Studies" or "European Studies," without the need for an emphasis on "Italy" as an intermediary field or "filter." The only exceptions to this might be certain historical or literary studies that focus on the period after 1700 or 1800.

Here one takes a clue from Cyril Toumanoff, a longtime professor of history at Georgetown University, whose views influenced many young scholars, including a future American president. A specialist in Armenian, Georgian and Russian history, Toumanoff was fond of observing that everything of historical note emanated from the Mediterranean. He lived long enough to see the dissolution of the Soviet Union and the restoration of an earlier name to his native city, Saint Petersburg.

This book is not an apologia for secession, nor is it an ethnocentric encomium for Sicily or Sicilians. It is about people, past and present. It is about studying the legacy of a particular place over its last three thousand years of civilization. Sicily has much to teach us, and the lessons to be learned are universal.

We are all Sicilians.

Sicily is more than sunshine, *cannoli* and *caponata*. Humanistic disciplines like history bring us distasteful facts along with the more enticing ones. As much as your authors praise the land of their ancestors, they criticize its flaws. In this book the reader can expect blunt, dispassionate commentary, beginning with the very first chapter.

That is because the only productive study of anything is based on fact. We shall presume that anybody reading these words wants to learn something which, in turn, can be taught to somebody else. Anything worth teaching is worth teaching well.

We will not presume that you are an expert on Sicily, or even very familiar with it. The third chapter recounts Sicily's story in its most essential outlines, from the mists of antiquity to the present century.

This volume was written to provide you with useful, accurate, unbiased information. It is essentially a menu from which you can choose the books most relevant to what you wish to teach.

Context is important, but excessively ideological or philosophical analysis has been kept to a minimum.

Objectivity is a holy grail for those who write about society, culture or history. You have a right to know if the authors of this kind of book have any social or political affiliations that might cloud their views. The authors are not associated with any public agency or institution in Italy, nor have they ever been employed by, or received funding from, any organization or government. They do not belong to any political party or movement in Italy. They do not represent any government. Any opinions expressed in this volume are those of its authors alone and do not necessarily reflect the views held by those whose works are mentioned in these pages.

Let's begin our journey.

MAPS
and
FIGURES

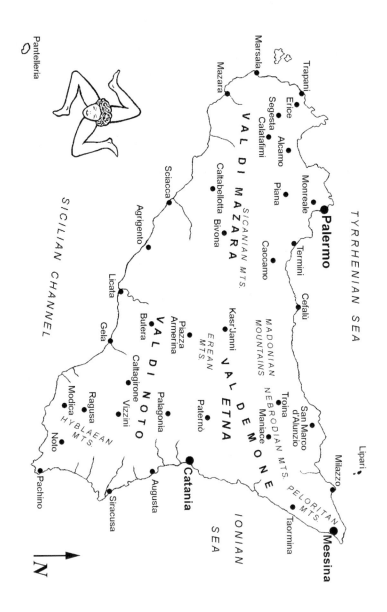

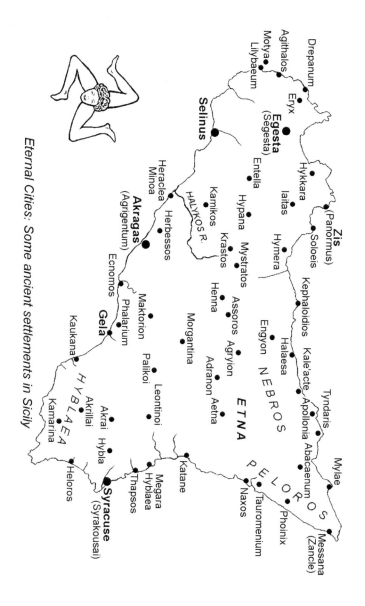

Eternal Cities: Some ancient settlements in Sicily

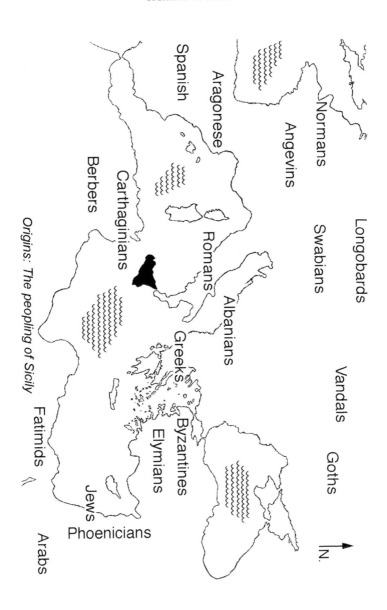

Origins: The peopling of Sicily

Regnum Siciliae: The Norman-Swabian Kingdom of Sicily

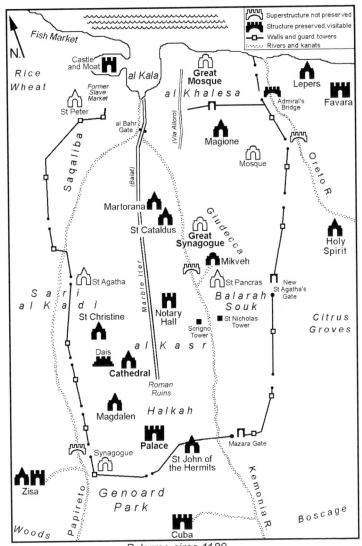

Palermo circa 1180

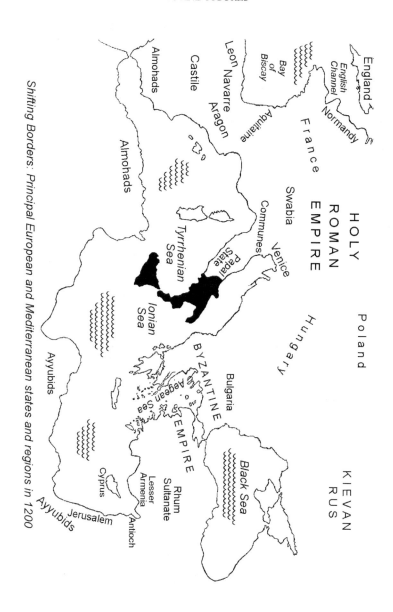

Shifting Borders: Principal European and Mediterranean states and regions in 1200

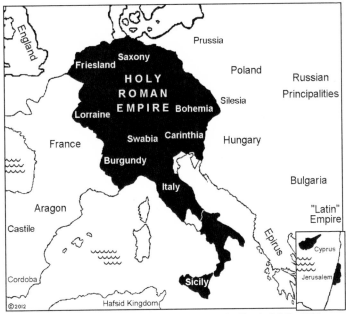

Greatest extent of Hohenstaufen dominion under Frederick II - 1230

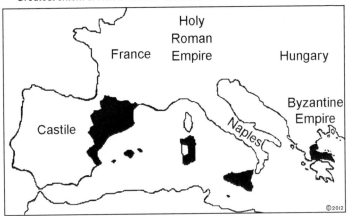

The Crown of Aragon in 1330

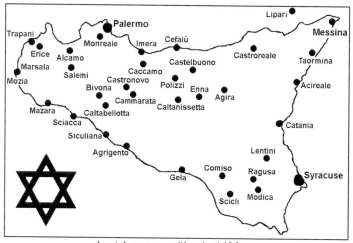

Jewish communities in 1490

Domains of Charles V circa 1550

Jewish Districts of Syracuse and Palermo

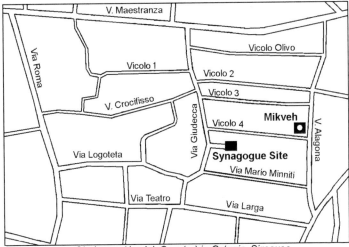

Giudecca (Jewish Quarter) in Ortygia, Siracusa
Great synagogue site is St John's Church. Mikveh at Via Alagona 52.

Palermo's Jewish Quarter, Souk (now Ballarò Market) and Kemonia Spring
Great synagogue site is San Nicolò da Tolentino Church. Mikveh under Jesuit cloister.

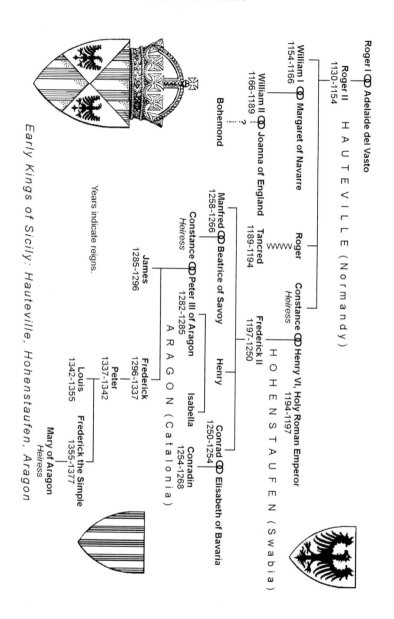

Early Kings of Sicily: Hauteville, Hohenstaufen, Aragon

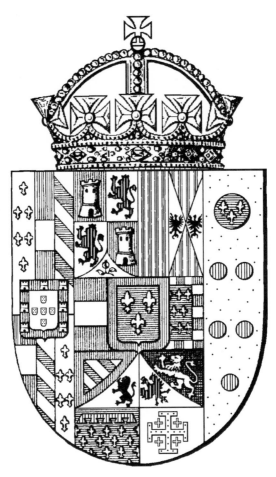

The coat of arms of Naples and Sicily beginning with the reign of Charles de Bourbon (later Charles III of Spain) in 1734. This was the coat of arms used in the Kingdom of the Two Sicilies until its demise.

NOI CARLO III.

Per la grazia di Dio Re di Castiglia, Leone, Aragona, delle due Sicilie, Gerufalemme, Navarra, Granata, Toledo, Valenza, Galizia, Majorca, Siviglia, Sardegna, Cordova, Corfica, Murcia, Jaen, Algarves, Algezira, Gibilterra, delle Ifole Canarie, delle Indie Orientali ed Occidentali, delle Ifole e Continente del Mare Oceano; Arciduca d'Auftria; Duca di Borgogna, Brabante, Milano, Parma, Piacenza, e Caftro; Gran Principe Ereditario di Tofcana; Conte di Abfpurg, Fiandra, Tirolo, e Barcellona; Signore di Bifcaglia, e Molina, &c. &c.

RA le gravi cure, che la Monarchia delle Spagne, e delle Indie, dopo la morte dell' amatiffimo mio Fratello il Re Cattolico Ferdinando VI. Mi ha recato, è ftata quella, che è venuta dalla notoria imbecillità della mente del mio Real Primogenito. Lo Spirito de' Trattati di quefto Secolo moftra, che fi defideri dall' Europa, quando fi poifa efeguire fenza opporfi alla Giuftizia, la divifione della Potenza Spagnuola dall' Italiana. Vedendomi perciò nella convenienza di provveder di legittimo Succeffore i miei Stati Italiani

The Pragmatic of 1759 founded the House of Bourbon of the Two Sicilies, the dynasty that ruled until 1860

Italian states in 1859: The Kingdom of the Two Sicilies was annexed to Italy in 1860

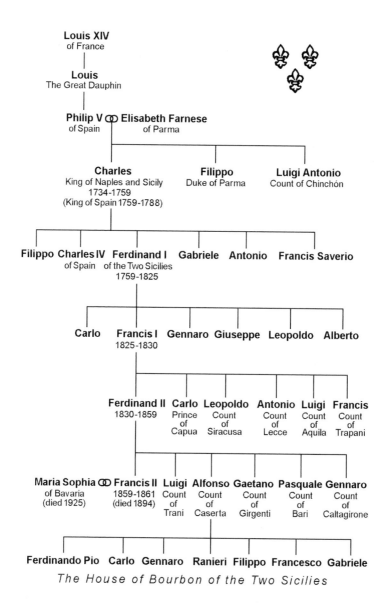

The House of Bourbon of the Two Sicilies

The Bourbon dynasty of Francis II, who ruled the King-dom of Naples and Sicily (the Two Sicilies) until 1860, shared the Capetian lineage of Charles of Anjou.

Maria Sophia Wittelsbach (shown), consort of Francis II, was Queen from 1859. Elisabeth Wittelsbach, the wife of Conrad and mother of Conradin, was Queen from 1250 to 1254.

ROYAL GIFT, AND THE KNIGHT OF MALTA, two valuable JACK ASSES,

WILL cover Mares and Jennies at MOUNT-VERNON, this Spring, for Five Guineas the Seafon.
The firft, is of the moft valuable Race in the Kingdom of Spain.—The other, lately imported from Malta, by the Way of Paris, is not inferior.——ROYAL GIFT, (now 5 Years old) has increafed remarkably in Size fince he covered laft Year—and not a Jenney, and fcarcely a Mare to which he went, miff d.——THE KNIGHT OF MALTA will be 3 Years old this Spring—is near 14 Hands high—moft beautifully formed for an Afs—and extremely light, active and fprightly.—Comparatively fpeaking, he refembles a fine Courfer.

Thefe two JACKS feem as if defigned for different Purpofes equally valuable.—The firft, by his Weight and great Strength, to get Mules for the flow and heavy Draught.—The other, by his Activity and Sprightlinefs, for quicker Movements on the Road.—The Value of Mules, on account of their Longevity, Strength, Hardinefs and cheap keeping, is too well known to need Defcription.

MAGNOLIO

Stands at the fame Place, for FOUR POUNDS the Seafon.—The Money, in every Cafe, is to be paid at the Stable, before the Mares or Jennies are taken away.---No Accounts will be kept.----Good Pafture, well enclofed, will be provided, at Half a Dollar per Week, for the Convenience of thofe who incline to leave their Mares, and every reafonable Care will be taken of them ; but they will not be enfured againft Theft or Accidents.

JOHN FAIRFAX, OVERSEER.

Mount-Vernon, March 12, 1787.

Advertisement for services of donkeys given to George Washington by King Charles III and by Emmanuel de Rohan-Polduc, Grand Master of the Order of Malta

St Peter's, the first Catholic church in New York, was built in Manhattan in 1785 with funds from Charles III.

Mosaic icon of Thomas Becket at Monreale

A gold reliquary pendant made at Canterbury given to Queen Margaret shows her being blessed by Saint Thomas Becket

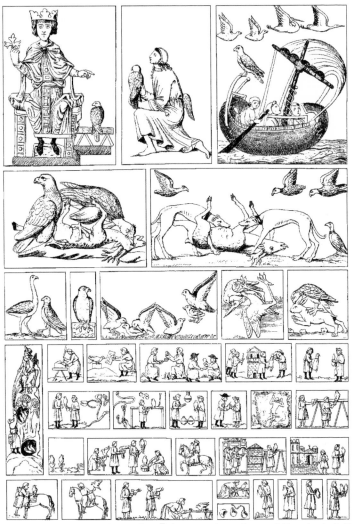

*Engraving based on the falconry treatise of Frederick II,
one of the most important scientific works of its time*

1
FOUNDATIONS

Sicily is — to use an overused word — unique. Although its modern culture is essentially Latin, like those of Italy and Spain, from which it has been ruled, its trimillennial history is an eclectic mix that has left us some interesting artefacts in language, cuisine, art and, most obviously, architecture, for Sicily was touched by civilizations from Europe, Africa and Asia. Perhaps the most compelling reason to study Sicily is the island's multicultural heritage. It is not, however, the only reason.

Telling Sicily's Story

Unlike other parts of Italy, such as Tuscany, Sicily has not historically enjoyed the benefit of much of her history or literature being presented in English. Moses Finley and Denis Mack Smith, respectively an American and a Briton, wrote the first major, general English-language history of Sicily, a work in three volumes, in 1968. For reasons we shall explain, very few histories of Sicily published in English are written by Italians.

Only in 2015 was the *Rebellamentu di Sichilia contra Re Carlu,* a memoir about the Sicilian Vespers rebellion of 1282 written in Middle Sicilian, finally published in English; this defining work of literature was composed on the initiative of John of Procida around 1290.

The work of women has usually been ignored; the novellas of Maria Messina, who wrote during the Fascist era, have only recently found their way into English.

By way of comparison, the polymath Dante Gabriel Rossetti rendered the first translation of the *Contrasto,* a poem of the Sicilian School written early in the thirteenth century, for publication in Britain during the reign of Queen Victoria. This was long after the poetry of his medieval namesake had been published in English in various translations and editions. Rossetti, despite his recent Italian ancestry, was raised in England and spoke Dante Alighieri's language flawlessly.

The Academy

In stark contrast to Rossetti, very few Italian-born professors teaching the humanities here in Italy ever achieve anything like fluency, or even an acceptable proficiency, in English.

But, you ask, what about those myriad programs in Florence for visiting students? With the obvious exception of courses intended to teach the Italian language, most of the lectures for visiting (non-Italian) students in study-abroad programs sponsored by foreign universities in places like Florence and Rome are presented in English by visiting Americans, Britons or Canadians. In the typical scenario, University X in New York sends its own (English-speaking) professor to Florence to teach the students from University X about the Renaissance. The students participating in the study-abroad program of University X in Italy are not thereby attending an Italian university but an American university that has a teaching center (or "annex") in Italy. This is not a new idea; the classic examples are the British School at Rome and the American Academy in Rome, both founded over a century ago.

Would that the predicament were confined to communication. The Italian academy is a rather peculiar environment where one hears that the Italian constitution of 1948 is clearly superior to those of Britain and the United States! In Sicily, one sometimes encounters the bizarre claims that a meeting of barons in 1130 was the first parliament in Europe, and that the massive Allied invasion of 1943 owed its success to support by the Mafia.

Unfortunately, such ideas can become dogma in a nation where, from a young age, students are still taught history through rote memorization rather than freethinking inquiry. In Italy, undergraduates studying history and literature are only rarely required to write essays or term papers until, at the conclusion of their course studies at the end of three or four years, they are expected to compose a "thesis."

The *modus vivendi* of the Italian academy is a reflection of Italian society as a whole.

Italy was born geographically divided in 1860 and then found herself socially divided after 1945, with the effects still felt in Italian politics today. Unlike, for example, the United States, which has confronted the ugly side of its history reflected in such developments as the enslavement of Africans and the massacres of America's indigenous peoples, Italy has never come to terms, historiographically speaking, with things like the bloody unification war of 1860-1861 or the evils of the resulting unitary state, specifically the repression of free speech in Italy, colonial genocide in Libya and Ethiopia, and (last but not least) Fascism. Unexpectedly confronted with unflattering facts by a foreign voice, an Italian raised and educated in Italy may respond instinctively and defensively, suddenly uttering uncharacteristically patriotic platitudes in advocacy of beleaguered *Italia*.

In fairness, it must be said that this kind of "defense mechanism" is not unique to Italians. Every nation's past bequeaths its citizens a few unpleasant things we would rather forget, and Italy is no different, but we cannot deny history if we hope to learn about it (or from it). Education must be based on evidence and analysis, not emotions and self-interest.

In Italy, it may be difficult to ascertain whether an apologist's position is rooted in sincere belief (regarding something like the Garibaldi myth) or mere propaganda (thus ignoring facts such as the genocide perpetrated by Mussolini's government in Africa).

Pride is good but facts are better.

As this book is intended chiefly for educators working *outside* Italy, an exhaustive analysis of the strengths and weaknesses of Italy's academy and professoriate lies beyond the scope of our discussion. For the more curious reader, a number of articles published in the international press address such topics as clientelism, corruption, nepotism, sexism and the question of academic integrity.

"Higher Education in Italy: A Case for Change" in *The Economist,* 15 November 2008, page 32, states that "...this week news emerged of a university rector who, the day before he retired on October 31st, signed a decree to make his son a lecturer. At Palermo University, as many as 230 teachers are reported to be related to other teachers." In "The Ins and Outs: Italians are deeply anti-meritocratic" in the same publication, 9 June 2011, the term *raccomandazione* (preferment) is explained.

A more recent report is "Seven Professors Arrested in Florence University Nepotism Row" by Thomas Kington, published in *The Times* (London) on 27 September 2017. For a description of student life at Italy's public universities, see Domenico Pacitti's "No Holiday in Rome" in *The Guardian* (London), 8 October 2002. For the high prevalence of plagiarism in Italian universities, see Wendy Sutherland-Smith's *Plagiarism, the Internet, and Student Learning: Improving Academic Integrity* (2008), pages 88-89.

Bizarre as it may seem, most of these practices are accepted as ethical in Italy.

Sadly, not a single Italian university was listed in the top hundred in the *Times Higher Education World University Rankings* for 2018 (published on their website), nor for the immediately preceding years.

These conditions need not be enumerated *ad nauseam,* but they explain why many talented scholars born in Italy are compelled to seek greater opportunities at universities abroad for graduate study and professorships.

A wry but insightful glimpse of life in Italy is to be found in *The Italians* (2014) by John Hooper.

Publishing

Why are there not more books in English that facilitate a study of Sicily and its culture? Apart from the reasons already cited, several factors are at work.

Except for literary fiction, few of the books mentioned in this guide are works in translation. Considering, as a ready example, the books that focus on history, there are practical reasons for this, and here we'll cite the most conspicuous among these.

Most obviously, historians educated outside Italy typically have a broader, less myopic, world view of Sicily than Italians in Italy tend to have, a reality which sometimes results in more insightful scholarship by foreigners; anglophone nations like the United Kingdom and the United States boast multicultural societies full of immigrants that make it easier for people raised there to understand, and write about, Sicily's polyglot Middle Ages than (for example) a Palermitan who has never met a Sicilian-born Jew in Palermo.

As we have seen, deficiency in the presentation of certain modern topics is equally personal; out of embarrassment, Italians are sometimes reluctant to address subjects like Fascism and Italy's role in the Second World War as clearly or objectively as a non-Italian would. This is unsurprising if we consider that in 1981 the Italian government refused to license the theatrical release of *The Lion of the Desert,* a major motion picture (starring Anthony Quinn, Oliver Reed, Rod Steiger, Irene Papas, John Gielgud and numerous Italians) depicting civilian massacres in Italian-occupied Libya during the Fascist era. The national censorship finally ended when the film was broadcast on Italian satellite television in 2009, but the subject still is not taught in Italy's schools. (Today, obviously, anybody with an internet connection can find accurate information about such topics.)

Your students have a right to learn the whole story, not just part of it.

Some Italian publishers recognize the superiority, or at least the competence, of foreign scholarship. That's why David Abulafia's biography of Frederick II and John Julius Norwich's books about the Normans in Sicily have been published in Italian. For comparison, try to imagine a biography of Eleanor of Aquitaine or a history of Plantagenet England authored in Italian by a hypothetical Maria Siciliano or Vincenzo Palermo being translated for publication in Britain, where the book then becomes the standard work on its subject.

This is hardly a novel notion; Donald Matthew expressed a similar thought in 1992 in his "Modern Study of the Norman Kingdom of Sicily" (in *Reading Medieval Studies,* volume 18).

An exception to this idea seems to be Steven Runciman's fine book on the Sicilian Vespers. Here some Italians prefer Michele Amari's slightly slanted version.

Confronted with high publishing costs and uncertain profits, the typical academic or trade publisher in Britain or the United States is, understandably, reluctant to invest in a costly translation in addition to the other expenses entailed in bringing a book to market. Whereas an author of non-fiction might be paid a minimal advance and, thenceforth, a small percentage from future profits, a translator is more likely to be paid a flat fee, which may be considerable for a book running to a hundred thousand words. There is also the expense of purchasing foreign-language rights to publish the translation of a work already published in Italian.

An obvious, cumulative effect of these phenomena is that very few books published in English about Sicily are authored by Sicilians. Only very rarely do Italian university presses publish books in English, although an article written in English occasionally appears in a scholarly journal published in Italy.

It has long been the case that many who love Sicily most have no ancestral connection to it. Indeed, there is a paucity of books on Sicilian culture and history written by Italian descendants outside Italy (e.g. Italian-Americans).

For the most part, our emphasis shall be placed on books that you can obtain rather than academic papers published in scholarly journals, although the latter will be mentioned from time to time.

In purely logistical terms, is it practical to assign work that requires a class of twenty or thirty students to all go down to the university library to consult the lone copy of a certain anthology or journal? Under copyright law, it may (or may not) be acceptable to photocopy and distribute a few pages from such a volume, but that presumes its benefit to your students. The uneven quality of anthologies (edited collections) and academic journals, which in recent years have published papers that are ever more recondite and pedantic, is considered in Chapter 6. To this category may be added some of the dissertations that are adapted to monograph form, even a few of those published by "prestigious" academic presses.

This brings us to the question of the quality of the work published by such presses (publishers) generally.

Compared to some other fields and regions (e.g. the medieval history of England), so little has been published in English that pertains *directly* to Sicilian Studies that it is fruitless to debate the perceived merit of one press over another, even for what are essentially academic monographs subjected to some form of peer review, a process useful for the works of professors seeking tenure. For example, no university press (e.g. Oxford) or major non-university academic press (e.g. Brill) has ever published a monograph in English dedicated exclusively to the Sicilian language; even Professor Frede Jensen's magisterial translations of some poems of the Sicilian School were published by a small "independent" press. If, either for your students or for your institution's library, you are seeking to acquire the *only* English translation of a certain prose chronicle from Middle Sicilian or the *only* guide to Modern Sicilian grammar (see Chapter 9 for both), the prestige of the press that publishes it is not likely to influence your purchasing decision, nor should it.

Certain "mainstream" academic presses are sometimes reluctant to publish works for which they believe there is an extremely limited market. The superlative English translation of the *Annals of Saint Vaast* by Steve Bivans, a scholar of Norse history, was published privately in 2017.

Peer review is sometimes problematic. How many scholars who speak English as their mother tongue are proficient enough in something as arcane as the medieval form of Sicilian to review a work in translation for accuracy? Anglophone scholars consulting such texts usually rely on published Italian translations.

Even books published by the most prestigious presses contain errors. Moreover, some topics, such as the *Risorgimento* (Italian unification) and the Mafia, engender such eclectic views and information that there cannot be said to exist a single, "canonical" paradigm for studying them beyond, one hopes, a diligent application of the most essential epistemology.

A related matter concerns credentials. Some authors are full-time, tenured professors, whilst others are independent scholars. Among the former was Denis Mack Smith, and in the latter category we find such luminaries as Sir Steven Runciman. Here again, it is the work itself that counts.

Proponents of "open access" argue that scholarly work should be available for free download if public funding has defrayed the cost of the research that results in a certain monograph or paper. This publishing model is still being developed. For now, few of the works described in these pages are free.

Ideology

Apart from certain literary works that appeared beginning in the nineteenth century, not enough has been published about Sicilian society to discern in it much more than subtle ideological trends.

One may well debate whether this or that history of Sicily published since 1800 reflects authorial views that are progressive, reactionary, liberal, traditionalist, conservative, conformist, Catholic, anticlerical, monarchist, socialist, republican or (more recently) postmodernist, however each of these terms is defined. Neither the Reform nor the Enlightenment made great inroads into most of what is now Italy, where Waldensians and Jews were persecuted.

Although ideologies and labels abound, it is difficult to discern more than the faintest outlines of any real trends in the current, factionalized study of Sicilian history. The field is whatever any particular author or educator wants it to be. It evolves continuously. Perhaps that is a good thing.

Unlike the United States and Britain, Italy does not boast lofty, unifying, centuries-old constitutional principles so laudable that they are studied in other countries. Instead of a "Second Renaissance," republican, quasi-socialist Italy has spawned widespread cynicism and indifference.

Benedetto Croce, who died in 1952, was the last Italian historical ideologue to influence more than a few people, though generally not for the better; he was a rabid apologist for nationalism and Fascism.

There exists no Sicilian ethos, ideology or philosophy. "Sicilianism" is not Judaism. Nowadays few Italians seek their social identity from either the church or the state. They may look to their families, upon whom they must rely in the absence of a firm social infrastructure, but people are not their grandparents; families themselves have evolved, with some twenty-five percent of Italian children born outside marriage.

The social environment is nothing if not fragmented. One meets Sicilian Catholics and Buddhists, conformists and freethinkers. Lifestyles vary, as do views of traditional "Italian" institutions. There is a growing population of immigrants from Asia and Africa.

Unless you are teaching a highly specialized course in a very specific area, sophisticated ideology probably does not need to be considered at great length. That Karl Marx was no fan of Giuseppe Garibaldi is, at best, a peripheral thought.

Looking back further in time, in antiquity we find Hellenism and in the Middle Ages multiculturalism. In these pages we shall contemplate the greater implications behind such developments when it is necessary.

Considering that the first historical survey of the entire life span of the Kingdom of Sicily, from 1130 to 1860, was published only in 2015, it is unsurprising that little material is available on such topics as multiculturalism, gender studies or Sicilian queens, let alone something expressly "ideological."

For now, it is the most essential teaching material, the foundation, that is needed. To propound anything more arcane would be like proposing cosmetic plastic surgery to a patient who requires emergency care for a broken leg.

How ideology is interpreted and taught shall be left to you, the educator.

As we noted in the preface, an academic colleague whose career is deeply invested in the general concept of "Italian" studies (at a time when some universities are downsizing their Italian departments) may be resistant to the idea of studies that focus on the history, literature or language of a specific region of Italy south of Rome, much as somebody specialized in "Spanish" studies may oppose the study of subjects related to Catalonia or Navarre.

Apart from entrenched, longstanding biases of that kind, one of the reasons such attitudes persist is because many experts in various Italian subjects (such as medieval literature) are unfamiliar with Sicily. If you are one of them, the simplest solution is to read this guide, along with the books mentioned in it that are most relevant to your discipline, and then get to Sicily for a familiarization tour of some of the places mentioned in Chapter 12.

Except for history and literature since around 1800, a study of Sicily or its culture need not even be associated with an Italian department. As we shall see in Chapter 3, Sicily has been a kingdom unto itself, and at times it has been an integral part of the Byzantine, Fatimid, Aragonese and Spanish empires. That's why Modern Sicilian sounds more like Catalan than Italian, and has words derived from Arabic.

Pedagogy and Methodology

Depending on the focus of your course, lessons on topics involving Sicily may be associated with Italian studies or with Europe and the Mediterranean more generally. We confess to a preference for the generalist approach because it places our island into a global context and because it appeals to a wider audience.

A course dealing with the Normans or Fatimids might benefit from a lecture or two on the connection of these civilizations to Sicily.

It is presumed that most of the professors or other educators reading these words have enough background and experience to know how to outline and teach an introductory or survey course on a humanistic subject. Except for a few generalities, our suggestions focus on the subject itself and the resources available rather than suitable teaching methods.

Considering the material available, lectures and class discussions, and perhaps a simple essay, are more effective than dogmatism or memorization.

There is no single, perfect approach. The pedagogy or methodology you choose will depend on your students and your objectives. A third-year university student may expect to use the course or seminar as a springboard for further study of Sicily, or to complement what she has already learned about Italy and the Mediterranean. An adult-education student, conversely, may be seeking little more than an introduction to an interesting place that, perhaps, he plans to visit. There may be specialized interests in literature, music, art or cuisine. A travel agent who plans trips to Sicily will benefit from a greater knowledge of the place and its people. For secondary- school students, Sicily may be part of a general course on Italy, the Mediterranean or multicultural societies.

Admittedly, the kind of study program advocated in this book is better suited to the essential needs of undergraduates than to the requirements of graduate students working on a thesis or dissertation. The latter scholars, one imagines, would understand enough Latin, Italian, and perhaps German or French, to consult resources in those languages directly.

It is exceptional to constrain students to purchase more than two books as required reading for an introductory course, but reasonable to expect them to read one or two others if necessary.

The elder of this guide's authors vividly recalls an undergraduate survey course on tsarist Russian history (taught by the late Brenda Meehan) for which the text was an updated edition of Nicholas Riasanovsky's lengthy tome, supplemented by Ivan Turgenev's *Fathers and Sons*. It was an effective combination. The term paper was a succinct analysis of Turgenev's book and the final exam was an essay.

That course of so many years ago was one of the inspirations for the idea behind this book.

Perhaps you are reading this to teach only yourself, to find recommendations for a few good books and a path to learning. If so, the authors commend you for your initiative and wish you an enlightening journey. This is the kind of guide they wish were available when they began their serious study of Sicilian history over three decades ago.

Recommendations

We certainly do not suggest that you select any book for a course, or recommend it to your students, without first reading it. This volume is merely a guide.

Over the course of a number of years, we have personally examined every book and academic paper mentioned in these pages.

A fundamental underpinning in the teaching of any subject, including those that fall into the broad category of social science, is sound epistemology, a concept closely related to the historical method, itself rooted in the Socratic method. While most authors embrace such principles, some do not.

In formulating this kind of guide, with its suggestions, reviews and critiques, one is confronted by hard choices. Most of the books which are not mentioned here fall into one of two categories.

No book is perfect, but some are far less perfect than others. Certain books are simply mediocre, so flawed that they cannot be recommended, even with a dangerously large dose of equivocation. Such books sometimes sow more harm than good. Rather than writing "diatribes" against those works, we have elected simply to refrain from mentioning them. A few professors reading this may have experienced for themselves the vitriol that sometimes taints otherwise useful academic criticism and book reviews, and we have chosen to avoid it here.

Another challenge concerns books that are out of print. An older publication, perhaps in the public domain, may be available as a digital download or through print-on-demand; this was the case of Lynn White's *Latin Monasticism in Norman Sicily,* published in 1938. Some books in our collections were purchased used. A category of books we were forced to eliminate from consideration are recent short-run publications (typically fewer than eight hundred copies) that are simply unavailable anyplace, even in some major libraries to which we have access. Granted that this could change from one day to the next if a publisher decides to reprint such a book, there were a few titles that, over the course of several years, we could not obtain from any vendor in any format, even as ebooks. Obviously, we could not evaluate or review a book we could not even find!

In some instances, you will find a suggestion for two books on the same topic, and we may explain why one is superior to the other.

Several authors were kind enough to provide us with electronic manuscripts of their forthcoming books. Only a few of the books considered in this volume exist exclusively in electronic format (presently lacking a print edition).

The student seeking to study a topic or sub-topic further will find ample bibliographies in most of the books mentioned in these pages. Many of those specialized works of research are published in Italian, French, German or Latin.

This guide is not intended to promote our books over those of other authors. Some text, most notably the history in Chapter 3, is extracted from our own books, rather than those of others, because copyright laws do not permit us to quote such an extensive passage (some twenty thousand words) from another historian's book. As regards recommending our own titles, most of our books are, at present, the *only* books published on certain topics (Sicilian genealogy, Queen Margaret of Sicily, translations of the Jamsilla and Ferraris chronicles), and therefore we could not exclude such works simply because we are their authors.

Where this book presents forthright observations about situations here in Italy, the commentary is based on the authors having lived in Sicily for decades.

In seeking an intellectual equilibrium, the authors of this book have chosen to remain aloof of the dissonance and feuds that poison the academic sphere. Some differences are rooted, if only ostensibly, in ideology, but others are motivated by little more than rabid envy. Thus one hears a Sicilian who owes her professorship in Italy to a preferment, rather than merit, declare with unbridled hubris that an Oxbridgian scholar "knows nothing" about a medieval subject in which he is an acknowledged expert.

Objectivity is important. As we stated earlier, this book is meant to provide you with accurate, reliable, unbiased information.

Digital Resources

Despite the existence of some excellent websites and applications, including a few that teach the Sicilian language interactively, the ephemeral nature of digital data hosted on a server made it impractical to recommend these by name and address, much as we would like to. There are, however, other problems in this area.

Educators are gently reminded that many public websites and other internet-based resources do not always reflect reality. Beyond the possibility of a website's publisher (or writers) deliberately presenting misinformation, certain "legitimate" electronic publications fail to consistently edit for accuracy. This is especially true of online encyclopedias that are "open source," meaning that anybody (or almost anybody) can edit them subjectively and anonymously (or even spitefully), with some entries being more accurate than others.

Despite the highly deceptive appearance of all websites being "equal," an anonymous publishing/editing environment of this kind cannot be compared to a "community of scholars," or even to a book (or article) written by an identifiable author and edited by a publisher's experienced staff.

By way of example, it would be difficult to ascribe much credibility to a site or page about the Bourbons of Naples that, among its attributions (citations), overlooked or purposely ignored the two books written about this dynasty by Sir Harold Acton. In an environment characterized by anonymity, frequent copyright infringement and verbatim plagiarism, it is difficult to ascertain the actual source of what you are reading. You could even be reading a slightly-modified excerpt from one of Acton's books without knowing it because a citation is lacking. That is just one of the potential pitfalls in recommending web-based resources to students.

The Sicilian Diaspora

Sicily is the world's island, and in many ways being Sicilian is a state of mind.

Very few of the millions who visit Sicily each year have personal, ancestral connections to the place. For those who do, the books mentioned in these pages will serve as a primer for further discovery.

In some cases, what one reads and what one sees may change longstanding misconceptions. There is much to learn and see throughout Italy, but somebody whose ancestral roots reach into the Sicilian soil will discover (or self-discover) more vestiges of familial heritage in Sicily than elsewhere.

Every voyage begins with a thought.

2
CONCEPTS

The underlying foundation for most of what we shall present in these pages is history. It is the common thread woven into the multicolored tapestry that is Sicilian Studies. Or a background against which everything else is set. History is the orchestral theme or (in popular music) the instrumental backing track that enhances the vocals, which would otherwise sound as if they were sung *a cappella*.

Nothing in the teaching of subjects involving Sicily need be unduly opaque or complex, although, as we shall see, learning (or re-learning) about certain details may make for uncomfortable reading for some.

History Wars

Today's historians broadly distinguish between traditional "political" history, with its emphasis on great events, macro economics and important personages, and "social" history, with its attention to trends, lifestyles and the greater number of ordinary people. Academics who teach in universities tend to pay more attention to social history than do the generalists who write popular, bestselling books about major wars, pivotal events or famous figures. The two approaches are not mutually exclusive, and they occasionally cross paths. They are also quite fluid, evolving with new research and changing perspectives.

In Sicily, women's studies, popular literature and folk art are obvious reflections of social history. Accounts of the Punic Wars or the War of the Vespers are examples of political history. The way we define history is less important than the way we study it and teach it.

Historiography

Several views of history (one hesitates to call them "movements") color the modern perception and presentation of Sicilian history and culture. Some have fallen by the wayside.

Until recently, Sicily's social history was largely ignored by academics. Here in Italy it still is, though that need not concern us excessively.

Corrective revisionism based on a competent application of the historical method (mentioned in the previous chapter) has "set the record straight" regarding Sicily's role in Italian history. Here several points spring to mind, and you may occasionally encounter these as well as others.

In antiquity, the Romans disparaged the Carthaginians, Vandals and Goths. These peoples and their contributions to society are now being recognized. The Greeks who once ruled most of southern Italy were spared the worst vilification because their society and culture, and even their deities and architecture, were closely imitated by the Romans.

With the demise of the Norman-Swabian Kingdom of Sicily (the eponymous island along with most of the Italian peninsula south of Rome) in 1266, the Angevins of Naples disparaged the defeated. Even the Sicilian language was derided, and by 1400 Tuscan had become the literary vernacular throughout most of what is now Italy, even if local languages like Sicilian and Neapolitan were still widely spoken. This set the stage for further decline. True, the Sicilians successfully revolted against the Angevins in 1282, but the rebellion's aftermath found the island ruled from Spain for the next few centuries.

After 1860, Italian unification emphasized a standardized, conformist view of the nation's history. Although scholarly studies about the medieval Kingdom of Sicily found their way into arcane academic journals, a *de facto* censorship discouraged the publication of widely-disseminated biographies of, for example, Roger II and his grandson Frederick II, two of the greatest kings of their era.

This was not a formal, stated policy, nor was it part of a complex conspiracy. It was, however, deliberate, part of a general trend, and it fostered some stubborn clichés, such as the idea that the south of Italy was less literate than the north (in fact the literacy rate throughout the country was uniform at around fifteen percent) and more backward (an appendix in this volume lists some technical achievements of the south before 1860), if not poorer (when it was looted in 1860 the Neapolitan treasury boasted gold reserves greater than those of all the other Italian states combined and until 1880 most Italian emigration was from the north, not the comparatively affluent south).

By 1900, emerging industrial technologies were being developed in the north, in places like Turin, while the south was left to languish.

Under Fascism, an unabashedly totalitarian regime, the unitary state instituted formal censorship, and eventually the teaching of English was banned in public schools. The Fascists' propagandistic *Enciclopedia Italiana* credits Giuseppe Garibaldi's friend Antonio Meucci (a Tuscan who immigrated to New York in 1850), whose name was scarcely known in Italy before 1930, with inventing the telephone, something Italian children are still taught today. The same encyclopedia entry vilifies Alexander Graham Bell and Elisha Gray as charlatans.

Italian unification itself is a tenuous concept that is still challenged from time to time in the socio-political realm. In reality, the undeclared unification war of 1860 was anything but what was traditionally taught to Italian school children. This propaganda was later contested by foreign historians like Robert Katz and Denis Mack Smith.

Following the Second World War, the Allies occupying the defeated nation granted women the right to vote and made the King of Italy, Umberto II, sign the decree establishing Sicily as an autonomous region, a status comparable to what we see with Scotland and Catalonia. In 1946, the king was exiled following the referendum ousting the monarchy but Sicily still has its regional autonomy.

"Only in a free nation," said Voltaire, "can history be taught accurately."

Feminism

Incredible as it may seem, the history of Italian women still is not studied very much in Italy, at least not as a subject unto itself. Few of Italy's universities present much at all in the field of gender studies, even within the context of generalist topics like the *Risorgimento*. (This is partly a result of Italian historians' emphasis on political history over social history.)

Even when the subject is broached, the study of the status of women in Italy often overlooks significant details. For example, the legal codes promulgated by Roger II and Frederick II outlawed rape (though chiefly of nuns) in the Kingdom of Sicily. These laws fell into disuse, if not abeyance, with the fall of Frederick's dynasty during the thirteenth century. Only in the twentieth century did the Italians again make rape a crime. Frederick's laws, the Constitutions of Melfi, permitted divorce, a right destined to reappear in Italy quite belatedly, in 1970 (sic).

Sicilian women probably enjoyed a higher level of literacy and education under the Hautevilles in 1170 than they did under the Savoys in 1870. It is certain that they had greater individual rights in the thirteenth century than in the nineteenth.

Multiculturalism

In common parlance the term is much politicized, but in this book *multicultural* simply describes the presence of people from several distinctly identifiable cultures in the same society at the same time, all accorded equal rights. Here there is no perfect paradigm, and Sicily's polyglot society was far from utopian, but the period in question generally runs from 1070 to 1266.

During the Norman-Swabian era the Kingdom of Sicily, and particularly the island of Sicily, boasted a diverse population of Arabs, Normans, Germans, Italians ("Lombards"), Byzantine Greeks and Jews. Islam, Judaism and two branches of Christianity (Orthodoxy and Catholicism) were practiced. This is what we mean by *multicultural*.

Literacy levels were high, among women as well as men, and although there was feudalism personal rights were guaranteed by the solid legal codes enacted in 1140 and 1231.

Sicilianism

The study of specific regions which were once sovereign nations is sometimes (though not necessarily) associated with independence movements and rabid ethnocentrism. That is not the case of this book, which has no political objective.

However, we do not define Sicily and its culture "dialectically" in relation to the unitary Italian state that emerged after

1860. Unlike nations such as France and Spain, which achieved unification centuries earlier, Italy, like Germany, is the product of a nineteenth-century movement. Before then, one referred generically to *Italians* and *Germans* based on geography and language rather than fixed political borders. We are inclined to agree with Metternich that, until unification, Italy was essentially a geographical expression.

Sicily had its own language and culture long before there was a modern Italy. Neither Garibaldi nor Mussolini could change Sicily's ancient or medieval history.

Whatever historians choose to write, the overwhelming majority of today's Italians are far from fervently nationalistic. Italy's chronically chaotic domestic politics, with its plethora of political parties, is anything but unifying, while the nation's stagnant economy renders job-seeking more urgent than flag-waving. As we have noted, many leave the country of their birth to seek opportunities abroad, where they raise their children as "hyphenated" Italians; there are now more Italians in London than in Bologna (but fewer than forty thousand Brits in Italy).

For better or worse, Italian nationalism proved rather ephemeral, and it was not destined to survive the Second World War. In a book described in these pages, Rick Atkinson mentions that the women of Licata threw rubbish from their balconies onto the heads of the Italian soldiers taken prisoner as the defeated men were marched along the town's narrow streets by the victorious Americans in the summer of 1943.

Cosmopolitanism

That the Sicilians, though part of a culture that has been essentially Latin for centuries, are descended from various peoples is a fact confirmed by the analysis of genetic haplogroups (DNA). By comparison, certain regions, like Iceland, were historically more isolated; that was not the case of medieval Sicily in any anthropological, geographical or cultural sense. Even Sicilian cuisine has been influenced by this diversitude.

Yes, Sicily, like Tuscany, Umbria and Lombardy, can be studied as a region of Italy, but it offers the curious student much more than that. The authors of this guide strongly advocate the view that the lessons to be gleaned from a study of our island transcend "conventional" studies of any single nation.

Sicilian Studies, as we shall see, is a rather broad field that offers much possibility for exploration.

Three Millennia

Sicily's history is lengthy and sometimes complex, and only a specialist can be presumed to be very familiar with it. No single book can make anybody an expert on Sicily, but the next chapter offers a general historical overview.

3
SICILY

Let us suppose, for the sake of productive conversation, that you are considering a course about some aspect of Sicilian history, society or culture but, as it happens, you are not very familiar with our island. This lengthy chapter was written with you in mind.

Even if you *are* familiar with Sicily, this capsule history may serve to draw your attention to a few key facts. Three thousand years of history have bequeathed us a great deal of information.

Most importantly, this chapter serves as a ready reference for many of the subjects mentioned in subsequent chapters. The timeline (Appendix 1) complements this narrative, which is extracted from our books *The Kingdom of Sicily* and *Women of Sicily*.

Backstory

At 25,711 square kilometers (9,927 square miles), Sicily is the largest island in the Mediterranean and the largest of the Italian Republic's twenty political regions, slightly larger than Piedmont. For comparison, Wales covers 20,780 square kilometers and Massachusetts 27,340. In addition to the island of Sicily, the region includes a number of coastal and volcanic islands. For many centuries, Malta and Gozo were ruled from Sicily.

The highest peak is Mount Etna, western Europe's largest active volcano, at a variable 3,329 meters (10,922 feet) above sea level, followed by rocky Pizzo Carbonara (1,979 meters) and several other summits in the Madonian range, and forested Mount Soro (1,847 meters) in the Nebrodian range. All of these peaks are covered with snow for at least two months of the year, Etna usually for three or four. The Hyblaean Mountains of the southeast are scenic but not nearly so high. The Peloritans in the northeast, near Messina and Taormina, form an impressive ridge.

The mists of prehistory leave us with only imprecise dates, but cave drawings at Addaura, outside Palermo, and Levanzo, in Sicily's Aegadian Islands, have been dated to approximately 9000 BC (BCE), coeval with the monumental structures at Göbekli Tepe in Asia Minor.

The Proto Sicanians, Sicily's earliest indigenous civilization, constructed Europe's first megalithic temples on the islands of Malta and Gozo beginning around 3800 BC.

The Sicily known to the ancients was an idyllic refuge of forests populated by deer, boar, hare, hedgehogs and striped cats. Sparkling streams full of fish meandered through lush meadows. Tempestuous Etna dominated the east, overlooking the scenic Nebrodian, Peloritan and Madonian ranges, where fir trees reached like spires toward the heavens. The Nebrodies take their very name from *nebros,* the Greek word for the deer that thrived there. Eagles and hawks soared above them, while grouse and pheasant populated the bush lands of the foothills.

Over time, rampant deforestation took its terrible toll. First, the rapacious Romans destroyed trees to make room for grain cultivation. Later, the Aragonese needed timber for ship building. In more recent centuries, overpopulation and mediocre land management have claimed many woodlands. There is far less precipitation than there was in the Middle Ages (or even fifty years ago), and the average annual mean temperature is higher.

The inception of Sicily's Bronze Age can be dated to around 2500 BC, preceded by the Copper Age a few centuries earlier.

Sicania

By around 2000 BC (BCE), Mycenaean and Late Minoan (Cretan and Aegean) cultures were present in isolated eastern localities of Sicily, especially near the Ionian coast, and by this time Malta's last temple builders, identified with the Tarxien Culture, had left Malta, with some perhaps settling in south-eastern Sicily, in effect returning to the land of their ancestors. The Ausonians, an Italic people, traded with the Aeolian islanders and other peoples in the northeast, around Messina.

At some point before 1200 BC the indigenous Sicanians were joined by the Italic Sikels in the east, and the Elymians, of Anatolian origin, in the northwest. These three societies seem to have coexisted peacefully, though our knowledge about them is sketchy at best. Sicily's name comes to us from the ethnonyms for two of these early civilizations, hence *Sicania* and *Sikelia*. By this time, the Iron Age had already begun in the Greek world.

Sikelia

The seafaring Phoenicians, who are usually identified with the Biblical Canaanites, founded Carthage in northern Africa around 840 BC (BCE). Within a few decades, the Phoenicians and Greeks began to colonize Sicily as part of their burgeoning empires. Of course, there were Phoenician influences long before this, their alphabet being perhaps the most obvious example, forming the basis of the Greek, Etruscan and Latin systems; some of the art they left in Sicily bears Egyptian motifs.

The Phoenicians established emporia in the island's west, especially at Motya (Mozia), Zis (now Palermo) and Solunto.

The Greeks founded colonies at Naxos (near Taormina), Agrigento, Catania, Selinunte, Messina, Gela and, most importantly, Syracuse (Siracusa).

The Elymians, whose major cities were Egesta (Segesta) and Eryx (Erice), readily assimilated with the Greeks.

The Sicanians had less affinity with Greek culture but seem not to have resisted colonization to a great degree. Except for excavations and necropoli, the tangible vestiges of their civilization are few, but the remains of a Sicanian temple rest atop the mountain overlooking Cefalù.

The Sikels, on the other hand, fought a long series of battles against the Greeks, and the last isolated pockets of Sikelian resistance, led by the man to whom Greeks ascribed the name *Duketios* (Ducetius), were defeated only around 440 BC.

It wasn't long before the prolific Greeks colonized most of Sicily and most of the Apennine Peninsula south of Rome, a territory roughly contiguous to the Norman Kingdom of Sicily and the Bourbons' Kingdom of the Two Sicilies, but these colonies in *Megara Hellas,* or "Greater Greece," eventually emerged as sovereign, independent cities. United by language and culture, they were often divided by politics.

The *Siceliots* (as the Sicilian Greeks were known collectively) were frequently at odds with each other, and this sometimes led to war. Most often, these rivalries pitted cities like Selinunte and Agrigento against Syracuse, which was Sicily's largest, wealthiest metropolis throughout antiquity.

It is generally believed that the Greeks brought viticulture and oleoculture to Sicily, but wild grapes and oleasters thrived on the island since time immemorial, and a few native varieties are cultivated today. However, it is beyond doubt that the Greeks greatly augmented what agriculture they found.

A case in point is the Kalamata olive. An exemplar in the Hyblaean Mountains is genetically identical to Greek cultivars, descended from stock originating in the Peloponnese and introduced in Sicily nearly three thousand years ago. (One of this book's maps is dedicated to traditional Sicilian olive cultivars.)

Selinus (Selinunte) took its name from *selinon,* the wild celery that grew there. Artichokes, their English and Italian names deriving from the Arabic *kharshùff* rather than the Greek *cynara,* are indigenous; pistachios were brought from Asia.

It was not only their agriculture that the Greeks introduced in Sicily, but their philosophy and mythology. Representing triangular Sicily's three geographic extremities, the three-legged triskelion, or *trinacria* (shown at the beginning of this chapter), bearing the head of Medusa in the middle, is a Greek symbol; it may have inspired a similar emblem that came to identify the Isle of Man.

The center of the Greek city, and the focus of local activity, was the *agora,* which survives today in the *piazza* or town square. Even the architecture of Sicilian cemeteries, tight rows of tombs outside town, reflects ancient Greek and Punic tradition. The Greeks have left some impressive temples, particularly those at Segesta and Agrigento, and two particularly large theatres at Taormina and Segesta.

The word *democracy* comes to us from the Greeks, but so does the word *tyrant.* The government of Greek cities varied from time to time. Administration, and the very philosophy of governing, might change at the whim of a single ruler or a few oligarchs; not all were very enlightened. Yes, life in a Greek community could be unpredictable.

Yet Greek culture has given us Sophocles, Aristotle, Plato, Aesop, Thucydides, and (in Sicily) Archimedes, Empedocles, Theocritus, Philistus, Stesichorus, Timaeus, Aeschylus, Diodorus Siculus, Epicharmus, Charondas and Gorgias.

When Phoenicia fell to the Chaldean Empire in 612, Carthage became the Phoenicians' major city. With the emergence of Punic Carthage as perhaps the wealthiest and most powerful metropolis in the Mediterranean, the Siceliots turned their attention to this new adversary. What followed was a complex series of wars over several centuries involving a tangled web of alliances with participants as far away as Persia.

In 480 the Carthaginians, exhorted to fight the Greeks by Xerxes of Persia who had won victories in Greece, were defeated by Gelon of Syracuse at the first Battle of Hymera. The Persians, meanwhile, were defeated at the Battle of Salamis.

These campaigns did not succeed in expelling the vanquished from the island. In the wake of their crushing defeat at Hymera, the Carthaginians enlarged a few cities in the western third of Sicily inherited from their Phoenician ancestors. Lying near the Tyrrhenian coast between two rivers that ran through a valley protected by a ring of rocky mountains, the most important of these seems to have been called *Zis*. It is known to us as Palermo. Set upon a mountain, impregnable Eryx was also enlarged. This Elymian city became a major Punic bulwark.

The constant menace of war was a Sword of Damocles (to quote a fitting Syracusan expression) hanging over the Siceliots' heads. Peace was rare; the list of battles between Punics and Greeks would make for a lengthy catalogue.

But the Carthaginians weren't the only nuisance. A few years later, in 474, the Syracusans won a decisive naval victory over the Etruscans at Cumae, but the Etruscans' Latin successors, the Romans, would one day pose a far greater threat to

Greek hegemony. Visiting Syracuse some eight decades later, Plato suggested Sicily as a potential model for his utopian society, an idea that must have flattered the proud Siceliots.

Raging from 431 to 404, the Peloponnesian War was particularly bitter, leading to the Athenians' invasion of eastern Sicily where, fortunately, the Syracusans defeated them in 413.

Another Carthaginian war broke out in Sicily, lasting from 346 to 341. Following an ephemeral peace, there was a Carthaginian incursion into a few Greek areas in 311. Not without reason, the Siceliots were tiring of incessant problems with their contentious western neighbors.

In 310, the Greeks under Agathocles invaded some Carthaginian territories of the African coast. A treaty signed in 306 established the Halycos (Platani) River as the Greco-Punic boundary in Sicily. Such matters were inevitably complex; in earlier times the Siceliot city of Akragas, lying near this boundary, traded with Carthage, exporting olives and wines to the African city.

The remaining Greek territories in the peninsular part of *Magna Graecia,* their *Megara Hellas,* fell to the Romans following the Pyrrhic War. Our phrase "Pyrrhic victory" originated in Plutarch's description of some of the battles the intrepid Pyrrhus of Epirus won, so numerous were the lives sacrificed.

In 278, during this conflict, the Carthaginians (who were briefly, and anomalously, allied with Rome) laid siege to Syracuse until it was relieved by Pyrrhus, whose formidable forces then managed to occupy a few Punic cities in western Sicily for a short time.

By the time he departed their island, Pyrrhus was despised by the Greeks. The war's end a few years later marked Rome's emergence as a true power. The loss of the Italian peninsula dealt the Greeks a blow from which they would never recover. Their empire, such as it was, found itself deprived of the greater part of its western frontier.

Provincia Siciliae

Rome now coveted Sicily from across the Strait of Messina, where her Scylla faced the Greeks' Charybdis.

On the pretext of containing Punic influence in northeastern Sicily, where the Carthaginians maintained a garrison to keep an eye on the disgruntled Mamertines, the ambitious Romans invaded in 264 BC (BCE). The Punic Wars, which would continue for more than a century, were essentially a territorial power struggle rather than an ideological conflict, but the enmity was genuine and whoever controlled strategic Sicily would most likely emerge victorious. At stake was the entire Mediterranean, "the sea at the middle of the world."

In the southeast, in what was left of Greek Sicily, an effort was made to forestall annexation to either empire, Carthaginian or Roman. The Syracusans made a truce with Rome at the beginning of the invasion in 263, thus avoiding direct involvement in the First Punic War.

Akragas, instead, became the object of an interminable series of battles and sieges between Romans and Carthaginians. It was soon Punic in all but name.

The end of this war in 241 saw *Sicilia* become Rome's first foreign province, although a few years passed before this status was defined precisely in law.

The Syracusans' truce with Rome ensured peace and the guise of independence for half a century, but their subsequent support of the defiant Carthaginian leader Hannibal during the Second Punic War, which began in 218, brought an angry Roman army to their gates in 212. While characteristically deep in thought, Archimedes, the most brilliant mathematician and engineer of his age, was killed by a Roman soldier. Much of Sicily's Greek culture died with him.

Contested Akragas (Agrigento) was soon restored to Roman control. It was renamed *Agrigentum*.

The Romans appreciated Greek culture to the point of imitating its architecture and even adopting its deities under Latin names, but certain Greek advancements in the realms of science and technology were now stymied as Rome conquered the Greek regions. This has led to the modern belief that scientific knowledge might have developed more rapidly, and with fewer hindrances, had it not been for the growth of the Roman Empire and then the spread of Christianity.

Greek remained the island's chief vernacular language. Latin seems to have been spoken by a minority of Sicilians, but many were bilingual. Indeed, Greek became the second language of the Empire's intellectual and leadership classes.

Hannibal's defeat in 201 cleared the way for the ambitious Romans, who began to consolidate their influence in the central and western Mediterranean. The Second Punic War was over, but a third would follow, almost as an afterthought.

"Carthago delenda est," famously railed Cato the Elder. "Carthage must be destroyed!" His wish came true at the conclusion of the brief Third Punic War in 146.

Although the Romans imposed heavy taxes, Sicily flourished. The long Roman period was a prosperous one for Sicily. Indeed, the island emerged as an important crossroads in the sprawling Empire. Yet historians' references to it as "the bread basket of the Roman Empire" may manifest a slightly exaggerated perception, even though (as mentioned above) the Romans deforested many areas to make room for wheat cultivation.

The peace was punctuated by occasional unrest, such as slave revolts, the "Servile Wars." Eunus, a slave of Syrian birth, led a revolt in the Sicilian heartland beginning in 139, joined by another slave leader named Cleon. It took a Roman legion to subdue them. A second revolt, this time under Salvius, broke out in 104 in the western region around Segesta.

Under Rome, Sicily was to experience an unprecedented level of exploitation by a ruling class rife with greed and corruption. In 70, Cicero prosecuted Verres, the province's corrupt governor, who fled following the great orator's opening argument.

The first Jews of Sicily were present in Greek times; archeological evidence suggests that a community of the Samaritan sect flourished in Syracuse. More Jews arrived in Italy following Pompey's sack of Jerusalem in 63 BC. It has been suggested that the infamous Crassus, famous for defeating the slave army led by Spartacus, deported a number of Jews to Sicily, where they were enslaved, but evidence of this is sketchy.

There was unrest under the occupation of the island by Sextus, Pompey's son, in 44 BC, during the civil war that followed the assassination of Julius Caesar. After the defeat of Sextus in 36 BC, Octavian — who five years later found himself ruling the entire Empire — levied heavy taxes on Sicily.

Lasting from 27 BC until AD (CE) 180, the *Pax Romana* was a welcome interlude, yet it saw Jesus put to death in a localized disturbance around AD 33.

They have earned justified opprobrium for their brutal executions and their gladiatorial entertainment, but the Romans achieved much even as their imperfect society fostered countless contradictions. The evil of slavery existed, yet the blight of bigotry was largely banished. Peoples from around the vast Empire could become Roman citizens and many did. Rome brought writing to places lacking it. United by a common language, the inhabitants of disparate regions preserved many of their own local customs. Over time, there were emperors from Iberia, Africa and Asia Minor. The Romans' accommodation of this multiethnic panoply is something many modern nations would envy.

In some places the benefits of Roman rule were far greater than in others. Clearly, the Greeks had no need of Latin to achieve literacy, and neither did the Judeans, but written history in most of western Europe (including what are now Germany, England, France and Spain) arrived with the Romans. Here the *Germania* of Tacitus comes to mind; whatever its shortcomings, it filled a void in early historiography.

The Romans built roads and aqueducts. Concrete was one of their many innovations. They erected oval amphitheatres in Sicily while emulating the semicircular Greek theatre elsewhere in the expanding Empire. With its extensive mosaic pavements, the patrician villa outside Piazza Armerina is an abiding testament to Roman art.

Paul of Tarsus preached in Syracuse *en route* to Rome around AD 59. There may have been a small Jewish community there. At this early date, the Romans generally viewed Christianity as little more than an eccentric sect of Judaism.

The greatest influx of Jews arrived in Sicily during the decades immediately after 135, in the wake of the Romans' complete expulsion of the Jews from Jerusalem after Bar Kokhba's Revolt (which began in 132) during the rule of the Emperor Hadrian. This led to the *Diaspora,* from the Greek word for a "scattering" or dispersion.

Before long, Christianity came to be viewed as something more troublesome than Judaism, at least from what was then the prevailing Roman point of view. Christians were regarded with raw contempt. Saint Agatha was martyred in 251 and Saint Lucy suffered the same fate some fifty years later during the rule of the infamous Diocletian, who excelled at persecuting Christians.

Lucy's death in 304 came at the end of a long and wicked era. Emperor Constantine, whose rule began in 306, brought about a more tolerant treatment of Christians. His Edict of Milan of 313 legalized the open practice of the new religion. In 325 the Council of Nicaea established a uniformity in its fundamental precepts, and it was the Empire's official faith by 380. Before long, even some foreign peoples beyond the Empire's frontiers began to adopt Christianity. This included various Germanic tribes.

In Syracuse, the temple dedicated to Athena was converted into a church. Although this trend continued throughout the Empire, Syracuse Cathedral, dedicated to the *Theotokos,* epitomizes it better than most. Some theologians posit that it represents a simple transition among the Syracusans from the worship of a virgin goddess to the veneration of the virgin Mother of God.

In 395, following the death of Theodosius I, the Roman Empire definitively split into Western ("Latin") and Eastern ("Byzantine") administrations. Sicily began in the West but would vacillate between the two. Seven years later, the capital of the Western Empire was transferred from Rome to Ravenna. Eastern administration was based at Constantinople, the former Byzantium.

Myriad influences combined to eviscerate the mighty Empire, whose decline cannot be attributed to just one or two factors within or without. In the event, Sicily was one of the last provinces to fall to external forces.

The Vandals and Ostrogoths

In 378, a Roman army was defeated at the Battle of Adrianople, now Edirne in European Turkey, by the ravenous Goths, a Germanic people forced into Roman territory by the migrating Huns. Clearly, circumstances were changing, even if bureaucrats in Constantinople and Rome were initially reluctant to acknowledge the political implications of the debacle that took place at this outpost.

The Romans should have known better, for the new adversaries did not come from nowhere; they had been familiarizing themselves with Rome's culture for centuries. Some of the greatest Germanic military leaders were trained by the Romans, who permitted people on the fringe of the Empire to obtain citizenship. In an earlier time, such a man was Arminius, or Hermann, who won a decisive battle against the Romans in the Teutoburg Forest in AD 9 using what today would be called guerilla tactics. By the fourth century, the Germanic ranks were full of Hermanns who had received military training from the Romans.

When the Vandals, Sueves, Burgundians and other tribes crossed the Rhine in 406, the "Great Invasion" had well and truly begun. Alaric's Visigoths, or "Western Goths," sacked Rome four years later.

In 429 the Vandals occupied the Roman province of Africa, within striking distance of Sicily. Their arrival in his city the next year was one of the last things witnessed by a dying Augustine of Hippo, who would not have approved of the invaders' Arianism.

An invasion of Sicily in 440 was followed by a series of mass raids, but the sporadic Vandalic incursions were halted by the Byzantines over the next few years.

What followed was a succession of migrations and invasions throughout the moribund Empire. Attila's wandering Huns invaded northern Italy in 452. They never ventured as far south as Sicily.

Following the pattern established by the Visigoths, the Vandals sacked Rome in 455, returning to Sicily in a long series of raids in 461. By 468 they were masters of the island.

Compared to much of their African domain, Sicily was a verdant jewel, a precious emerald in a sapphire sea. Syracuse was the wealthiest city under their direct rule.

The Vandals left most of the existing administration in place but — true to their gentilic — they vandalized the synagogue of Syracuse, leaving it little more than a pile of rubble.

Odoacer deposed the last Western Roman Emperor in 476, and the beginning of the Middle Ages is usually dated from this time. The Vandal king Genseric, meanwhile, concluded a "perpetual" peace with Constantinople.

In 491 the Ostrogoths, or "Eastern Goths," achieved complete control of Sicily, ousting the Vandals, who retreated to their kingdom in Tunisia. The Goths made Ravenna their capital.

Like the Punic peoples before them, the Vandals and Goths suffered the fate of having their history written for them, in Latin, in a disparaging tone, by detractors. This has colored modern perceptions of these civilizations which are only now being corrected by historians.

While most of the peoples who conquered ancient and medieval Sicily left something of value behind, the legacy of the Vandals and Ostrogoths is more difficult to quantify, apart from some genes for blondish hair and blue eyes. Elsewhere, the Germanic languages are their legacy. Their rule defined a brief entr'acte, bridging the gap between what are now identified as the ancient and medieval epochs, but nobody living in the year 500 made such a distinction.

For now, their success seemed assured, but Sicily was a coveted gem. Only with the greatest effort might the Vandals and Ostrogoths keep the precious possession in their grip.

The Ostrogoth leader Theodoric the Great managed to keep his people unified against the Byzantine Greeks. His death in 526 brought an end to decades of peace.

Transition

The phrase "Dark Ages" reflects a modern bias, but it seems an apt moniker for what was widespread across Europe in the immediate aftermath of the fall of the Western Roman Empire. A few vestiges of the grandeur that was Rome survived in the eastern Mediterranean, where Greek was more widely spoken than Latin, in what has come to be known as the "Byzantine Empire."

Byzantine Greek culture was a stalwart pillar supporting the prosperous, literate society the northern Europeans found in Sicily in the eleventh century; Arab culture, which we shall meet shortly, was the other.

Ascending the Byzantine throne as "Roman" Emperor in 527, Justinian already had his eye on Italy. Nobody in Constantinople seemed willing to assent to a jewel — and a territory of strategic importance to commercial shipping — like Sicily remaining in Ostrogoth hands.

In 534 the Byzantine general Belisarius defeated the Vandals at Carthage and the following year he expelled the Ostrogoths from Sicily. The island was now officially part of the Byzantine Greeks' Mediterranean empire.

But the tenacious Goths did not succumb easily. The Ostrogoth leader Totila raided Sicily in 550 in an attempt to reclaim it for his people. This occupation — if it could be called that — was short-lived, really little more than a lengthy incursion. Totila's defeat by Byzantine forces at the Battle of Taginae two years later signalled the end of Ostrogothic influence in Italy.

The next wave of northern invaders, the Longobards, who became Italy's Lombards, stayed longer.

The Byzantine Frontier

The Byzantines eventually gained control over much of Calabria, Basilicata and Apulia, where Bari was their principal city. Their main sphere of influence was Italy's Adriatic coast. Ravenna and Venice were briefly in Byzantine hands, an influence reflected in the splendid mosaics of their cathedrals.

The Longobards invaded Italy *en masse* in 568 following Byzantine victories over the Ostrogoths in the bloody Gothic War. They handily confiscated rural areas, where they introduced something vaguely resembling rudimentary feudalism.

The Byzantines, for their part, were generally content to rule the more important centers, leaving the rest for the Lombards, but over the next few centuries there were occasional conflicts.

However, the decisive factor in Byzantine military strategy at this time had little to do with politics. For a generation or two, the problem was raising troops. An epidemic of bubonic plague in 541 decimated the population of the Byzantine Empire, rendering a reconquest of Italy from the Goths — and then the Longobards — all but impossible.

Significantly, the bishops in the Byzantine territories, and even in many of the Lombard ones, were under the ecclesial jurisdiction of the Patriarch of Constantinople, not the Pope of Rome. Equally important, the Byzantine cities implemented a variance of the Code of Justinian while in the Longobardic lands, at least initially, a form of Germanic law was enforced.

The Lombards never conquered Sicily, although a few arrived with the Normans. While the Italian regions under Lombardic control underwent the shift toward feudalism, Byzantine territories like Sicily retained a social and economic order more akin to the Roman model, at least for a time. Compared to the intellectual darkness that enveloped most of Europe, Constantinople was a beacon of learning and prosperity.

In 652 a small Arab force landed in Sicily but soon departed. Other raids followed. Mohammed had died in 632, and the Muslims' greatest assault on the island was yet to come. For now, the few Muslims in Sicily were traders.

The Emperor Constans transferred his capital to Syracuse for a few years beginning in 660. His main motive for the move was to establish a base for a Byzantine reconquest of peninsular Italy from the Lombards, but the fact that he considered the Sicilian city sufficiently important to substitute for Constantinople says much for its cultural and economic wealth.

Today we associate mosaics and other art with the Byzantines, but their society was much more than this, preserving a great deal of Roman and Greek learning in a changing world.

One thinks of scribes as monks, but the clergy, the "clerks," were not the only ones to perform this role. A number of manuscripts recording the work of great thinkers were preserved (in Greek) in the Byzantine Empire. Some were later translated into Arabic. Euclid's *Division of Figures* is an oft-cited example. In a few cases, the Arabic editions were the sources of later (Latin) translations when the Greek copies were lost or destroyed.

Venerated in East and West, Saint Agathus was one of the few Sicilian Popes (Bishops of Rome). It has been suggested that he began his religious vocation as a monk at one of the earliest Benedictine monasteries in Palermo, something which implies that in his time pockets of Western monasticism flourished in that part of Sicily amidst the Eastern majority. His pontificate lasted from 678 to 681. Agathus convened the Sixth Ecumenical Council at Constantinople in 680 to suppress the Monothelite heresy.

Although we have no reliable figures, such evidence as can be garnered suggests that general literacy in Sicily under the Byzantine Greeks was higher than in most of western Europe and that it increased further under the Arabs.

The Golden Emirate

Islam was the impetus for the spread of Arab power from east to west across northern Africa. The most popular modern definition of the demonym "Arab," which places any native speaker of Arabic in the same vague ethnic category, rings slightly simplistic to the ears of the medievalist. But Arabic is the language of the Koran, and in its nascent years Islam was inextricably linked to Arab culture. It was also a case of the Arabs having a written language, while some of the peoples they conquered did not.

Around 670 the Arabs founded Kairouan (Qayrawan), considered the first Muslim city of northern Africa, and by 700 the place we now call Tunisia was almost entirely under Muslim Arab influence. Before long, the great majority of Tunisians had converted to Islam and Arabic was the language that united them, but they were the descendants of Berbers, Carthaginians, Romans and even Vandals. For this reason, identifying the medieval Tunisians, or even the Moroccans, generically as "Arabs" is something of a simplification. Whatever one chooses to call them, there is no doubt that these peoples flourished as part of a larger Muslim society. Their influence eventually extended from Portugal to Pakistan.

The Muslims invaded Spain in 711, and Charles Martel stopped them at Tours in 732. Some years would pass before an invasion of Sicily was seriously contemplated.

In 827 Asad ibn al-Furat sailed from Tunisia with over ten thousand Arab and Berber troops, landing at Mazara in the western part of the island. Impressive as it was, this campaign was the result of Byzantine machinations and treachery as much as Arab ambitions. Euphemius, a Byzantine admiral and resident Governor of Sicily, found himself at odds with his Emperor, Michael II, and was exiled, so he offered the governorship of the island to Ziyadat Allah, the Aghlabid Emir of Kairouan, in exchange for his support. Euphemius was soon killed — reportedly by Byzantine soldiers in Sicily — and Sicily's Arab period began.

The Arabs met less resistance in the western part of the island than they would encounter in the east. In 831 Bal'harm (Palermo) was occupied by the Aghlabids, who came to refer to the city informally as *medina* and made it their seat of power in Sicily. This reflected a number of changes from the *status quo ante*. For over a thousand years Syracuse had been the island's most important city. Henceforth that distinction was to be reserved for Palermo.

There were several reasons for the preference of Palermo as the island's capital. It was closer than Syracuse to the Aghlabids' Tunisian capital, and farther away from the potentially troublesome Byzantines. Coming from the east, a Byzantine attack on the Syracuse region would leave time to notify Palermo of an attempted invasion.

In this magnificent city one of the largest souks became what is today the Ballarò street market (shown on the map of Palermo's Jewish Quarter). Its Sicilian name is thought to derive from the Arabic *Suk al Balari*. This may refer to much of the produce coming from *Bahlara*, a farming village near Monreale, or to *Ba'lat*, the name of Palermo's principal stone street.

By 903 the Arabs controlled all of Sicily, and Islam was the official religion. They tolerated Christianity and Judaism in Sicily, without encouraging either. In Sicily, the Arabs were rulers rather than colonizers, masters rather than leaders. Because Islamic law could be harsh to non-believers, many Christians converted, though precise numbers are not known and in the northeastern part of the island there were Byzantine monasteries throughout the thirteenth century. However, it must be said that Arab society and culture were advanced; under the Arabs Palermo emerged as one of Europe's richest cities.

In Islam, collections of *hadiths* containing *sunnahs,* or "laws," are very important. The Aghlabids advocated Maliki law, whose roots are to be found in the Sunni tradition. This says much about the legal system they brought to Sicily.

There were occasional conflicts between the predominantly Arab populations of Palermo, Marsala and Trapani, who controlled the island, and the Berbers who had settled in Agrigento and Sciacca to the south. To a great extent, these violent Berber revolts mirrored the situation in Tunisia, and worsened with the arrival of Fatimid rule after 909. They were, in effect, anti-Fatimid riots tantamount to a localized civil war that ended only following a siege at Agrigento, the Arabs' *Kerkent,* in 938.

Even though the Fatimids and their successors were Shiites they retained many laws established by the Aghlabids.

The Arabs introduced mulberries (for silk making), cotton, oranges, rice and sugar cane. The Fatimids are thought to have introduced the markhor, from which the Girgentan goat, with its distinctive corkscrewing horns, is descended.

The process of distillation, important in chemistry and in the making of spirits, was developed by the Arabs. They built water passages, *kanats,* under Palermo. Chess was played. Although some of these developments originated in India and China, it was the Arabs who brought them to Europe and the Mediterranean. Europe's first paper was made in Sicily, where Europe's oldest surviving paper document is preserved, and in Spain. Hindu-Arabic numerals were introduced.

Advances in mathematics were facilitated by the use of the new numerals, which trace their origin to Brahmi and Sanskrit. In Baghdad, the ninth-century Persian mathematician Abdallah Mohammed al Khwarizmi made use of this numeration system to simplify Diophantus' algebra, whose modern name comes to us from the Arabic *al-jabr wa'l muqabalah.* Hindu-Arabic numerals are not merely a simpler writing system than Roman numerals; they more clearly isolate concepts such as fractions and *zero,* whose Medieval Latin form, *zephirum,* derives from the Arabic *sifr,* "cipher," from a Sanskrit word. Khwarizmi's studies also encompassed trigonometry, astronomy and geography.

Schools were established for girls as well as boys, and literacy became the norm. Paper made it that much easier for the young students to master writing.

The Fatimids migrated their center of power to Egypt in 948, delegating the administration of Sicily to the local Kalbids. Before long, Madiyah (in Tunisia) was eclipsed by Bal'harm.

There were isolated pockets of resistance from time to time. The Battle of Rometta, a town on high ground to the west of Messina, may have begun as little more than a rare Byzantine revolt, but the arrival of thousands of troops from Constantinople in 964 suggests, instead, that this was the last city in Sicily to fall to the Arabs. Its very name means "fortress," from the Greek *erymata*. Emir Hassan al-Kalbi was killed during the fighting, but the Kalbids prevailed.

Three years later, Cairo, destined to become one of the most important Muslim-Arab cities, was founded by a Sicilian, Jawhar al-Siqilli, in the name of the Fatimids. By now, Palermo was a metropolis whose opulence was said by one visitor to rival that of Baghdad.

In 982, another Sicilian emir, Abu al-Qasim, was killed by Europeans at the Battle of Stilo, in Calabria, where the Byzantines joined the Arabs to defeat an invading army of the Holy Roman Emperor, Otto II.

The Arabs were prolific. They founded or resettled numerous fortified towns around Sicily. Most obviously, places whose names begin with *cal* or *calta* bear the mark of Arabic: Caltagirone, Caltabellotta, Caltanissetta, Calascibetta, Calamonaci, Caltavuturo, Calatafimi. Also in this category are places whose names begin with derivatives of *gebal* (Gibilmanna, Gibellina) and *recal* (Regalbuto, Racalmuto). This expansion, and the fact that wealthier Muslims could take more than one wife, explains how Sicily's population doubled or trebled during the few centuries of Arab rule. There were also many conversions to Islam, especially of young Byzantine women marrying comparatively affluent Muslim men. These facile conversions reflect the fact that in the Mediterranean many of the social differences between Muslims, Christians and Jews were fairly subtle well into the Middle Ages.

By the middle of the eleventh century the island's populace was divided about equally between Muslims and Christians, with Jews constituting the remaining population, less than a tenth of the total.

Kalbite society had its strictures for non-Muslims. As *dhimmi,* Christians and Jews were taxed more heavily than Muslims, and there were restrictions on the number of new churches and synagogues that could be built (Palermo's cathedral and some other churches were converted to mosques). Church bells could not be rung, and Christians could not read aloud from the scriptures within earshot of Muslims or display large crosses in public. Christians and Jews could not drink wine in public, though Muslims sometimes did so in private. Jews and Christians had to stand when Muslims entered a room and make way for them in the souks, streets and other public places. In Arab Sicily there was harmony and tolerance if not absolute equality.

Constantinople still lusted after Sicily, and it now seemed opportune to exploit a growing factionalization among the island's population. In 1038 George Maniakes, at the head of an army of Byzantines, augmented by Norse, Norman and Lombard soldiers of fortune, invaded the island from the southeast. The elite Varangian Guard was led by no less than Harald "Hardrada" Sigurdsson, the future King of Norway later defeated by the Normans in England.

The Normans were commanded by William of Hauteville. Nicknamed "Iron Arm," he reputedly killed the Emir of Syracuse with a sword in single combat.

This expedition might have been successful had Maniakes not been abandoned by his foreign knights. When he was recalled to Constantinople in 1042, Syracuse once again fell to Arab control. The Norsemen and Lombards seemed to have had no special interest in Sicily, but the appetites of the land-hungry Normans had been whetted by the rich island.

Few purely Arab monuments survive, most Siculo-Fatimid art being part of the later Norman-Arab movement that flowered around 1100. (The painted ceiling of the Palatine Chapel and the Islamic geometry decorating the exteriors of the apses of the cathedrals of Palermo and Monreale are typical of this syncretic style.) Among the exceptions are the baths at Cefalà Diana. Constructed during the tenth century, this is the largest purely Arab structure still extant in Sicily. Similarly, Taormina's Palazzo Corvaja was erected during the Arab period, although parts of it have been altered over time. Some *muqarnas* are preserved in a tiny section of the ceiling in the vestry of Palermo's cathedral, once used as a mosque.

Besides the kanats, feats of engineering left to us by the Arabs include some well-constructed bridges outside Corleone, Adrano and Roccamena.

In 1044, Hasan as-Samsam (Samsam ad-Dawla) was deposed but not killed, and it seems that he retained some local power. At this time, if not earlier, the Emirate of Sicily was divided into four *qadits* but there were rivalries among the *qaids,* the local governors. Had the *qaids* of the four *qadits* been united, Maniakes would not have run amok, virtually unchecked, for so long.

Sicily was tenuously united so long as the Kalbids ruled. Following the death of Hasan as-Samsam, the last of his dynasty, in 1053, three warring emirs divided control of Sicily. Ibn al Hawas ruled northeastern Sicily (Val Demone) from Kasr' Janni (Enna), Ibn at Timnah ruled southeastern Sicily (Val di Noto) from Syracuse and Catania, and Abdullah ibn Hawqal ruled western Sicily (Val di Mazara), a region which included opulent Bal'harm, from Trapani and Mazara. The word *val* did not refer to a valley, as is often presumed today, but to a *district*.

During this period of political chaos and localised power struggles the title of *emir* came to be abused, occasionally usurped by the *qaids,* who were actually leaders of large towns rather than entire districts, hence there was a nominal "Emir of Bal'harm" resident in the Favara palace in what is now Palermo's Brancaccio district.

What awaited Sicily was a society very different from what she knew under the Arabs.

Norman Sicily

On a clear spring night in 1061, an army of Norman knights crossed the Strait of Messina with their horses and weapons on specially-designed long ships reminiscent of those of their Viking forebears. The local garrison was taken by surprise, and before long the Norman conquest of Sicily had begun. The Arab soldiers should have foreseen the invasion, for the Normans had attempted such a landing the previous year.

If the military conquest bore the guise of Papal support, the knights themselves were earnest enough in their ambitions. The Normans were as hungry for Sicilian territory as the Papacy was covetous of Sicilian souls. Both would triumph in the end, firmly planting their banners in Sicilian soil.

The campaign was to be a cumbersome enterprise not unlike the one prosecuted by the Arabs during the ninth century. Robert "Guiscard" de Hauteville and his brother Roger, supported by a force of numerous Normans and Lombards, began with incursions into the Nebrodi Mountains, conquering towns populated by Greeks, Arabs or both. Only in 1071 did they reach Palermo, which they besieged following a combined amphibious and land attack. Fortified towns like Kasr' Janni (Enna) fell only because the local emir agreed to a negotiated surrender.

The Normans were descendants of Norsemen ("Vikings") who had settled on and around the Cotentin Peninsula in northwestern France in what came to be called *Normandy,* intermarrying with the predominantly Frankish-Celtic population they found there. In 909, Charles III "the Simple" ceded Normandy to the Norse chieftain Hrolf (Rollo), who became a Christian. Within a few generations a distinct ethnic culture had emerged, and with it the Norman-French language. In 1066, the Battle of Hastings, at which some Italo-Norman knights fought, led to the rapid conquest of England, but by 1140 the tax revenues of that entire kingdom were exceeded by those of a single Sicilian city, Palermo. Sicily's Hauteville dynasty was one of many landed Norman families to arrive in Italy during the eleventh century, generally poorer — but no less ambitious — than those who settled in England.

Robert left his sibling Roger, known to posterity as "Roger I," in charge of governing Sicily. What emerged on the polyglot island was a multicultural society of Normans, Lombards, Arabs, Byzantines, Jews and, eventually, Germans. Roger's first wife was Judith of Evreux.

For the first few decades of Norman rule, Sicilians were judged primarily by religious law, be it Muslim, Jewish or Christian. With the Church divided since 1054, new bishoprics were "Roman Catholic," under the Pope, rather than "Greek Orthodox," under the Patriarch of Constantinople. This led to interesting juxtapositions. In Palermo, during the middle of the twelfth century, the Greeks' Martorana was built next to the Latins' San Cataldo, both in a similar Norman-Arab architectural style, a syncretic movement born of eclectic influences that left some churches looking like mosques. Komnenian mosaic completed the picture.

Surviving examples of Norman-Arab architecture are nothing short of astounding. Palermo's Palatine Chapel, Cefalù's cathedral and Monreale's abbey, with its stupendous cathedral, cloister and Arab fountain, stand out, but they are not alone.

Roger I was succeeded by a son, Roger II, crowned as the first King of Sicily in 1130. Ten years later, his Assizes of Ariano unified the law into a single code partly rooted in the

Code of Justinian. Roger came to rule most of Italy south of Rome, and part of Tunisia.

This was the apogee of Sicily's golden age.

Roger II was a remarkable ruler for his time. He advocated learned science and developed a large zoo in the Genoard, the vast park and hunting ground to the immediate south of the Norman Palace and city walls, extending to Monreale. He died in 1154, the year that Abdullah al Idrisi, the court geographer, completed a survey known to us as the *Book of Roger*. Interestingly, Idrisi mentions the making of spaghetti at Trabia, east of Palermo, a fact which implies that it was indeed an Italian invention rather than an imitation of the Chinese food described by Marco Polo.

With Roger's death began the reign of his son, King William I "the Bad." In 1158, the Englishman known to Sicily's Arabs as *Qaid al Brun* (Thomas Brown), who served as treasurer at William's court, returned to England to reform the exchequer of Henry II, thus influencing European accounting principles. Brown used Hindu-Arabic numerals, which were later popularized in Christian Europe by Leonardo Fibonacci of Pisa.

Not everybody in William's realm entertained multicultural views. In 1161, Matthew Bonellus of Caccamo led some barons in a revolt rooted as much in ethnic bigotry as sedition.

In 1166, the reign of young King William II "the Good" began under the regency of his mother, Queen Margaret, who gave hospitality to the exiled kin of Thomas Becket. Rabbi Benjamin of Tudela visited Sicily in 1170, providing us with the most detailed medieval overview of Sicily's Jews.

It was William II who ordered the construction of hilltop Monreale Abbey in 1174, a few years before his marriage to Joanna Plantagenet, daughter of Henry II of England and sister of Richard Lionheart.

In 1184 the traveler Abu Hussain bin Jubayr visited Sicily and recorded his impressions, observing that the Christian women of Palermo "dress in the Muslim fashion," wearing headscarves, and wrapping themselves modestly in cloaks. Some types of jewelry, and perhaps ear-piercing, were commonplace. True, this was the prevailing mode of dress among Mediterranean Jews and Christians long before the arrival of the Muslims in Sicily. Nonetheless, it exemplifies a certain superficial commonality among the women of these Abrahamic faiths into Sicily's Norman era.

The Sicilian Crown was contested following William's death in 1189, claimed most prominently by Tancred, an illegitimate grandson of Roger II. For a few years Tancred Hauteville managed to impress the advantages of his leadership upon the unruly Norman barons of southern Italy. He died in 1194, leaving as the only potential, legitimate, immediate heir Constance, a posthumous daughter of King Roger II now wed to the Holy Roman Emperor Henry VI von Hohenstaufen.

The Swabians

We have seen that in the Middle Ages the ethnonym *Arab* came to refer to all Arabic- speaking peoples. By the same token, the gentilic *German* defined all of the German-speaking peoples of central Europe. The reference to the "Swabians" in Sicilian history is potentially misleading, as their number included a great many persons from German-speaking parts of the Holy Roman Empire well beyond tiny Swabia's borders. Frederick Barbarossa, the father of Henry VI, is perhaps the best known of Swabia's Hohenstaufens.

By virtue of the birthright of his consort, Constance de Hauteville, Henry VI claimed the Sicilian Throne in 1194.

Henry was crowned King of Sicily in Palermo Cathedral on Christmas of that year. The following day, in the Marches, the previously childless Constance gave birth, at forty-one, to a red-haired son christened Frederick Roger, subsequently known as Frederick II. Henry could not be present, but numerous witnesses were, making Constance's delivery one of the most crowded in history.

Henry VI now found himself in control of the island of Sicily and all of mainland Italy except for a central region (the Papal State) controlled by the Papacy, a situation the Pope and other sovereigns found disturbing — indeed overtly threatening.

Rarely contested in his German lands, the Emperor's power in northern Italy was not absolute. Eventually, a rivalry between factions developed, with the *Guelphs* (Welfs) opposing the *Ghibellines* (Hohenstaufen supporters who took their Italianized name from the Staufen fortress of Waiblingen). The Guelphs supported the Pope (and later the Angevins) against the Swabians. This undercurrent shaped Imperial politics in northern Italy for decades, and one day it would seal the fate of Sicily.

In 1198 the very young Frederick II von Hohenstaufen succeeded his father, Emperor Henry VI, to the Throne of Sicily. His first wife, Constance of Aragon, who like Margaret of Navarre came from what is now Spain, was an intelligent, strong-willed woman whose presence was eminently well-suited to such an important court as Frederick's.

Like his father, the enlightened Frederick ruled Germany and most of Italy, though he spent little time in Sicily. Frederick's bloodless "crusade" to the Holy Land — for he claimed the crown of Jerusalem through his second wife — was an exercise in diplomacy. He arrived in Palestine in 1229, securing control of the region not through military prowess and bloodshed but by skillful persuasion and delicate diplomacy, negotiating with the Muslims in Arabic, the language of the Koran. Frederick was crowned King of Jerusalem in the Church of the Holy Sepulchre. The island of Cyprus also came under his purview, though only briefly.

Promulgated in 1231, his Constitutions of Melfi are a benchmark of medieval European law, legalizing divorce as a civil right while outlawing rape. The king's justiciars, a roving court of circuit judges, sought to ensure justice around Sicily.

An avid scholar, freethinking Frederick was reputed to be brilliant. *Stupor Mundi* (Wonder of the World) was the Latin nickname given to the most powerful man of Europe and the Mediterranean, a polymath ahead of his time. In Papal circles he was regarded as a political rival, an iconoclast unimpressed by Rome's power.

By the middle years of the oft-excommunicated monarch's long reign, subtle, gradual changes were taking place as Sicily's Muslims converted to Christianity. They became Roman Catholic rather than Greek Orthodox; the latter were ever fewer.

Under the Normans most Sicilians had been bilingual; many spoke both Greek and Arabic, and some managed a bit of Vulgar Latin or Norman French. The vernacular language of the Sicilian Jews was a Maghrebi dialect rather similar to that spoken by the Maghrebim of Tunis, an esoteric "Judeo-Arabic" (shown in the tombstone of this book's back cover) written in Hebrew characters. Bilingualism was, in effect, integral to Sicilian society.

Now Sicily was being Latinized in every sense, and Ciullo of Alcamo composed poetry in the Romance language which was becoming the Sicilian tongue. This was a new Italic language embellished by Arabic, Greek and Norman French borrowings, and later recognized by both Dante and Boccaccio for its literary value. It has been suggested that, had Hohenstaufen rule of Italy lasted another few centuries, Sicilian, not Tuscan, might have become the national language.

Frederick founded one of Europe's first secular universities at Naples and he is credited with maintaining at least a semblance of the spirit of cultural diversity and intellectual curiosity that flourished at the court of his grandfather, Roger II. Nor was he forgotten in the German lands, where his building program included one of Europe's most magnificent Gothic cathedrals at Cologne — this despite a strained rapport with the local bishop.

But Frederick von Hohenstaufen's life was much more than this. He cultivated an interest in poetry and literature; the sonnet is said to have been born at his court. Falconry, ecology and efficient government were just a few of his obsessions. A king with an intellectual passion was as rare in the thirteenth century as it was in the twentieth.

Some of Frederick's exploits still elicit curiosity. His zoo, for example, included camels, elephants, panthers and what was probably the first giraffe ever brought to Europe — all gifts of the Sultan of Egypt, Malik al Kamil, with whom Frederick had negotiated his treaty in Jerusalem. He paraded these animals, to public amazement, during a visit to Ravenna in 1231.

Following Frederick's untimely death in 1250, the Throne was ascended by his son, Conrad, who died in 1254, leaving behind a young heir (Frederick's grandson), Conradin, in Germany. For a few years, the kingdom was ruled in young Conradin's name by Conrad's half-brother Manfred, one of Frederick's sons born outside marriage.

Frederick's heirs proved themselves far less adroit than he, even if Manfred and young Conradin ably managed to preserve the Hohenstaufen patrimony for a few years and were willing to fight to defend it. Sicilian independence came to an effective end with Manfred's defeat and death at the hands of Charles of Anjou at the Battle of Benevento in 1266, and young Conradin's beheading following the Battle of Tagliacozzo two years later.

The Arab-Norman-Swabian golden age had bestowed upon Sicily that rarest of treasures: multicultural tolerance. Its death was a human tragedy.

The demise of the Hohenstaufens led to the victory of the Guelphs over the Ghibellines in northern and central Italy. Poets like Dante, a Guelph, advocated their own vernacular tongue, which became Italian. Sicilian and Neapolitan survived, but neither would ever achieve Tuscan's prominence as a literary language.

Angevins and Aragonese

The new monarch sent his French justiciars, castellans and officers to Sicily, confiscating crown estates and giving them to his own avaricious nobles. Worse yet, whatever religious or ethnic diversity still existed in Sicily during the Hohenstaufen era effectively vanished when Charles of Anjou became king.

In the eyes of the Catholic Church, Charles is perpetually overshadowed by his pious elder brother, Saint Louis (King Louis IX of France), whose heart reposes in Monreale Abbey, site of his first European funeral *en route* to France in 1270. Significantly, Louis was known to have occasionally sided with Frederick II in the latter's conflicts with the Papacy.

Sicilian baronial opposition to Charles seemed to evaporate with the execution of brave young Conradin in 1268. Charles ruled Sicily from Naples until 1282, when a bloody uprising, the War of the Sicilian Vespers, expelled his Angevin troops.

The political reasons for this expedient war — traditionally if equivocally painted as a spontaneous popular revolt — were indeed rather complex, and there may have been a conspiracy behind it, instigated by Ghibellines, Pisans and Aragonese. At the same time, such incidents as the ready capitulation of Caltanissetta Castle to a small company of knights suggest that the rapid victory of the Sicilian barons resulted at least partly from the inadequate defense of fortified positions by the Angevins, who were probably overconfident.

The local nobility and John of Procida, an old friend of Frederick II, were certainly involved, but so were several European monarchs and perhaps even the newly-elected Pontiff. Byzantine interests were also at stake, as Charles was planning a massive invasion of Constantinople. In the event, he had to divert his military resources to Sicily, abandoning all hope of a conquest in the East. Consequently, the Greek Orthodox Church survived, whereas otherwise it might have been integrated into the Roman Catholic Church by 1300.

Whatever its impetus, by the time the rebellion was under way, it was unstoppable. Clearly, the defeat of the Angevins was a foregone conclusion once they had incurred the wrath of the seething Sicilian baronage.

In the wake of the Vespers, during which the Sicilians had slaughtered many of the Angevins on their island, the barons offered the Crown of Sicily to Peter III of Aragon, who gladly accepted. Peter's wife, Constance, was the daughter of Manfred Hohenstaufen (Frederick's illegitimate son killed at Benevento in 1266), and on that tenuous basis the Aragonese monarch was thought to be the best dynastic candidate for the Sicilian Throne since his sons carried Hohenstaufen blood in their veins. This led to the island being ruled, except for brief periods, from Barcelona, the Catalan capital of the Aragonese empire, and then Madrid, for the next few centuries.

That this new dynastic arrangement was antithetical to the very concept of an independent Sicily that supposedly encouraged the ruthless rebellion in the first place went unnoticed.

The Vespers, with Sicily claimed by two monarchs — Charles of Anjou in Naples and Peter of Aragon in Sicily — gave rise to the ironic toponym "Two Sicilies" because until now the Kingdom of Sicily included not only the island itself but most of Italy south of Rome. Neither Peter nor his hapless rival Charles would renounce his claim to the island of Sicily even though the former now held it in fact. Eventually the peninsular region would be called, more descriptively, the "Kingdom of Naples."

A treaty signed at Caltabellotta between the Aragonese and Angevins formally ended the hostilities in 1302, but occasional conflicts broke out between the two camps over the next few years. The Late Middle Ages found Sicily in the Aragonese (and Spanish) orbit rather than the Italian one. Endogamy prevailed as the island was enveloped by a stagnant monoculture. On the mainland, the Angevins forced Italy's last Muslims to convert to Catholicism or to leave Italy.

Casting off the Angevin yoke proved a mixed blessing for the Sicilians. Some detrimental effects were immediate. Taxation was increased. This included taxes on grain and everything else, and now there was the *collecta* or *donativo,* an arbitrary "one-time" tax which was not levied at regular intervals but could be decreed at royal whim to cover any exigency.

Now most of the forests that remained in Sicily were harvested (but rarely replanted) to provide wood for the Aragonese to build their ships, with the former woodlands turned over to grain production. In the process, the stately Nebrodi Fir nearly became extinct.

The zealous, jealous nobility, the same class that had incited the Vespers uprising in 1282, grew ever more greedy. Yet Sicily had no Magna Carta, nor a true parliament (despite widespread misuse of that term to denote any gathering of nobles), either to guarantee baronial rights or to rein in the barons as a class. Nevertheless, the Sicilian parliament, such as it was, met fairly regularly beginning around 1400.

In 1295 such a parliament was convened by Frederick, the younger brother of the absentee King James of Sicily (both were sons of King Peter of Aragon). At this session, the Sicilian baronage nominated Frederick, who was Sicilian by birth and upbringing, as their sovereign, and crowned him at Palermo the following year.

In 1347 ships arriving at Messina from the eastern Mediterranean brought the bubonic plague ("Black Death") to Europe. By 1400 more than twenty million Europeans had died from two major outbreaks of this disease. This catastrophe was a signal event in western European history, eventually bringing about the end of serfdom where it still existed.

In 1353, Giovanni Boccaccio's *Decameron* mentioned Palermo's Cuba palace. This was the beginning of a serious historical critique of Italy's medieval rulers.

Beginning in 1377, an interregnum led to feudal chaos, with large swathes of land laid waste as several baronial families, the so-called "Four Vicars," plundered Sicily until an Aragonese fleet led by King Martin arrived to restore order in 1392. Confronted with the dire consequences of their treason and thievery, the leaders of the Alagona, Ventimiglia and Peralta families turned on the Chiaramonte. Following a long coastal siege at Palermo, Andrew Chiaramonte, one of the chief usurpers, was beheaded in front of his castle, the imposing Steri, which became a royal residence.

Education was generally left to the schools of the religious orders. These monastic schools were not all seminaries or convents; aristocrats and even some tradesmen sent their sons to them. Except for nuns and noblewomen, literacy was now a male monopoly, but it was becoming the exception for either gender.

The unfettered nobility, of course, exploited the general illiteracy of Sicily's poorer classes to its own advantage. At some point after 1300 (and certainly by 1400), coincidental to the emergence of the Sicilian monoculture, a hopeless cycle of poverty and illiteracy began. This may not have been an intrinsic, causal effect of the disappearance of cultural diversity, but in the event social rights like divorce disappeared as Catholic zealotry took hold of society.

Historians debate the precise causes, and even the exact nature, of Sicily's denouement, but few question the decline in prosperity.

Alfonso V was crowned in 1416 and ruled for forty-two years; in 1442 the Sicilian and Neapolitan crowns were united under him. But for the most part the rulers remained in Spain; Aragon and Castile were united in 1479 to form the cornerstone of what was to become the Kingdom of Spain. Soon the Spanish kings would send governors and viceroys to administer Sicily on their behalf. Alfonso was a slightly more generous patron of learning and the arts than his immediate predecessors, and founded the University of Catania in 1434, but the Sicilians had to bear the cost of his petty wars against the maritime cities of northern Italy.

Constantinople fell to the Turks in 1453. The Hundred Years' War ended in the same year. The Middle Ages were at an end and the Renaissance was firmly on its course.

Sicily was virtually ignored by this movement, both artistically and philosophically. Prominent exceptions in the artistic sphere were Francesco Laurana, a sculptor who established a workshop in Palermo, and Antonello da Messina, a painter who used a mixed oil-tempera technique.

Well into the 1490s, while a new architectural movement was flourishing in northern Italy, in Sicily the churches and palaces of the fifteenth century were more medieval in appearance. The Catalan Gothic movement was the epitome of this; it was a style popular with the Aragonese, altered only slightly to accommodate Renaissance sensibilities. In church architecture, Sicily rarely experienced the true Gothic so much as a peculiar Romanesque imbued with Gothic details.

The merits of Sicily's lengthy Spanish period were equivocal at best. Misery was pervasive. Catholicism reigned supreme, with the Jewish minority (who we shall meet in the following section) eventually eliminated through deportation or forced conversion. This wanton disregard for individual liberties rarely saw so much as an inkling of the Reform or Enlightenment movements. The Inquisition ensured that religious freedom found no place in the social fabric of Spanish Sicily, or indeed anyplace in Italy.

The sacrosanct right to divorce was abolished. The rape statutes of the Constitutions of Melfi were all but forgotten, and rarely applied after 1300, leaving victims without recourse to law. Only in the last decades of the twentieth century would the Italians revisit these two issues, and then only following much public consternation.

Greeted with unbridled optimism in 1282, Spanish rule was to prove malignant, leaving Sicilian culture benighted. It would remain so until the eighteenth century, when the Bourbons undertook an effort at revival.

The Jews of Sicily

By 1400, the Jews were the island's only religious minority (though after 1470 Sicily saw an influx of Orthodox Christian Albanians fleeing Turkish expansion in the Balkans).

The Jews were involved with commercial trade, dying, tanning, metalsmithing and money lending. A handful were feudal landholders, effectively minor aristocrats. In the fifteenth century most of Sicily's best physicians were Jews, who during that period were certainly the best- educated segment of the population outside the nobility.

Syracuse boasted Sicily's first Jewish community, and its mikveh, carved into a limestone hypogeum, is probably Europe's oldest; the surviving mikveh under Palermo's Jesuit cloister may be older. (The sites of known synagogues and mikvehs of Siracusa and Palermo are indicated in one of this book's maps.)

In 598 the Patriarch of the West, Pope Gregory the Great, with the Papal Bull *Sicut Judeis,* ordered Sicily's bishops to protect the island's Jews from overt persecution and forced conversions. By the time the Arabs arrived there were flourishing Jewish communities in Syracuse, Messina, Panormus (Palermo), Mazara and elsewhere; many cities had a *giudecca,* or Jewish quarter.

In Saint John's Church in Siracusa's Jewish quarter is an inscribed stone thought to have belonged to a synagogue that stood nearby. In Agira, an *aron kodesh* (holy ark) in austere Gothic style dated 1454 is preserved in a church, having been retrieved from the local synagogue. In Siculiana a Jewish tombstone dated 1478 forms part of the baptismal font of the mother church.

Medieval Judaism in Sicily was initially Maghrebi, but by the fifteenth century it was essentially Sephardic.

In 1493, when the Spanish Crown forced the conversion or expulsion of Sicily's Jews, Palermo's Jewish community seems to have been slightly larger than Syracuse's, which was probably around five thousand. Estimates vary (typically counting households rather than persons), but into the fifteenth century as much as five percent of the Sicilian population may have been Jewish.

In 1474, in an incident that ominously presaged the cataclysm to come, some three hundred Jews were massacred at Modica for refusing to pray in a Catholic church. Sadly, such persecution of religious minorities would not be unknown elsewhere in Italy in the future; in 1655 the infamous "Piedmont Easter" saw over a thousand Waldensians brutally killed.

Contemporary observations regarding the Sicilian Jews were made by the rabbis Benjamin of Tudela in the twelfth century and Obadiah ben Abraham of Bertinoro in the fifteenth.

Some Jews were dissuaded from emigrating. Much like the *conversos* of Spain, they simply converted to Catholicism and remained in Sicily, assuming Christian given names at baptism and choosing new surnames. It is impossible to know precisely how many stayed, but it was probably less than half of the island's total Jewish population, and by some estimates only around twenty-five percent.

The horrors of the Spanish Inquisition nourished the reactionary elements of the prevailing social milieu, discouraging free thought in any form. Only in 1782 was the Inquisition abolished in Sicily. It had encouraged the kind of widespread suspicion, clannishness and clientelism for which — unfortunately — the Sicilians have come to be known. The Sicilian social culture we see today is largely the product of this period.

Spanish Sicily

After 1400 Sicily was governed, for the most part, from afar, yet the kingdom continued to exist even when its monarch might also wear other crowns and live in a foreign land. For example, the Holy Roman Emperor Charles V, a sovereign who reigned in the sixteenth century, was simultaneously the ruler of Spain, Sicily and other parts of Europe, as well as Spanish colonial territories in the Americas. The same monarch ceded Malta to the Knights Hospitaller as a bulwark against raids on Sicily by pirates from Africa and Turkey.

By 1500, the island was a bargaining chip of powers vying for control of the Mediterranean, but only for brief intervals of a decade or so did Sicily find herself ruled by dynasties other than those of Spain.

Following such an interval, during which Sicily was ruled from Vienna by Austria's Hapsburgs, it was returned to Spain (which by this time was ruled by the House of Bourbon) in 1734. Thus did Charles III, son of Philip V of Spain and Elizabeth Farnese of Parma, restore "home rule" to the kindred kingdoms of Naples and Sicily. It was during his enlightened reign that the city of Naples emerged as one of Europe's largest, wealthiest, most industrialized capitals, and at Italian unification the value of the gold reserves in its treasury exceeded that of all the other Italian states combined.

The "enlightened despot" was a rarity in any age, and Charles, who departed in 1759 to ascend the Spanish throne, was the last sovereign to reign over any part of Italy who could be described in such glowing terms. In 1735 he opened Naples to Jews for the first time in two centuries.

He led Spain through a brief economic and cultural revival, in the process suppressing the Jesuits and the Inquisition, actions mirrored in Naples and Sicily by his son, Ferdinand I. Charles supported the American revolutionaries in their War of Independence against the British, although his son, Ferdinand I, as King of Sicily, recognized the United States of America only in 1796.

The Bourbons managed to make their southern kingdom the most industrialized of the pre-unitary Italian states (see Appendix 2).

They wholeheartedly embraced their Italian realm, where Charles' descendants spoke Neapolitan as their mother tongue. One of these, the future Ferdinand II, was born at Palermo in 1810, being the last king to rule Sicily who was actually born on the island.

Seeking refuge in Palermo during Napoleon's occupation of the peninsula, Ferdinand I was encouraged by the British defending Sicily to grant a constitution. This he did in 1812. Feudalism was abolished. In its stead, the feudatories whose estates had the highest tax base were accorded seats in a Chamber of Peers similar to Britain's House of Lords.

Because the largest estates, the *latifondi,* remained in existence, the major landholders still wielded power, but certain areas used by the general public, such as major roads, became the property of the state. No longer was it possible for a baron to literally own an entire town.

With the help of astronomer Giuseppe Piazzi, who discovered the dwarf planet Ceres based on observations made from Palermo in 1801, administrative districts analogous to provinces were established based on topography, and some local officials would be elected. Initially, only literate landholding males were eligible to vote.

The state might create institutions, but the one most citizens knew best was the family.

Women

Until very recent times the few Sicilian women known to us as anything more than names were abbesses and aristocrats.

Most Italian marriages in the nineteenth century were arranged by the spouses' parents, or in any case contracted only with parental consent, just as they had been for centuries. The new vital statistics laws formalized the betrothal process.

Two customary practices among common folk represented opposite approaches to betrothal. Being *fidanzati in casa* was an engagement, sometimes before the future bride had reached the age of majority, where the parents of the future spouses would formally agree to the marriage.

Conversely, the *fuitina* was essentially an elopement in cases where the young woman's parents did not approve of the marriage, or perhaps could not afford to defray the cost of the wedding and therefore tacitly condoned the elopement. More precisely, in the *fuitina,* from the Sicilian word for "fleeing," the couple "escaped" together for a few days, and upon their return an immediate "reparative" wedding was deemed necessary to avoid further scandal because the young woman was presumed to have "lost her honour" during the sojourn.

Apart from these perennial practices, courtship, such as it was, might entail chaperones to ensure that the couple was never alone. On average, husbands were around eight years older than their young brides. Dowries and other details could make betrothals quite complicated.

The generic description of such a social hierarchy as "matriarchal" is specious at best. Nevertheless, the salient role of Sicilian women as wives, and especially as mothers, cannot be overlooked.

Two Sicilies

With Napoleonic France's defeat, Europe sought to restore some semblance of the *status quo ante bellum* to the Continent while laying the foundations of a cohesive policy that might prevent the likelihood of a major war breaking out again in the near future. This met with success if we consider that Europe enjoyed a respite from an extensive, multinational conflict for a solid century. Unfortunately, the Congress of Vienna failed to address most of the underlying social problems that existed *within* the signatory nations, things that fed a general discontent among citizens.

German unity of a kind was recognized in the form of the German Confederation. Italy, which Metternich famously described as being little more than "a geographical expression," remained a patchwork of monarchies ruled by the Pope, the Bourbons and the Savoys, with Lombardy and Venetia under Austrian control. Here the borders were nearly identical to what they were before the beginning of the Napoleonic Wars a quarter-century earlier.

Some frontiers had shifted; having seized Malta from the French (who had ousted the Knights Hospitaller), the British refused to restore it to the King of Sicily.

Ferdinand I was now free to decamp to Naples, which he much preferred to Palermo. In 1816, he abolished the Sicilian Constitution of 1812, justifying this caprice by uniting the states of Naples and Sicily that had been institutionally separate since the War of the Vespers. This new state, the Kingdom of the Two Sicilies, would need a new constitution, but Ferdinand had no immediate intention of granting one.

The Jesuits' general restoration in 1814 alarmed many, and not only in Europe. Across the ocean, John Adams wrote to American President Thomas Jefferson in 1816 that they "merited damnation."

The Last Bourbons

Francis I, who succeeded Ferdinand I in 1825, understood the importance of science and industry. He also knew a thing or two about politics. The new king granted a general amnesty for those involved in some recent revolts. This facilitated the return of political exiles.

Francis was dead by the end of 1830, succeeded by his Sicilian-born son, Ferdinand II. Revolution was in the air, its winds blowing across the Alps from France. The July Revolution of 1830 blew a gust of dissent into Italy.

In northern Italy, Giuseppe Mazzini, a young Genoan intellectual, advocated Italian unification under a republic where Papal power would be marginalized. As one can imagine, Mazzini was no more beloved by the Savoys in Turin than by the Bourbons in Naples.

One of the first acts of young King Ferdinand II of the Two Sicilies was a proclamation promising to guarantee justice to all citizens. He made an early attempt to root out corruption while encouraging fresh ideas by replacing jaded bureaucrats and aged personnel. In the end, this was only partly successful. However, cutting expenditures while encouraging commerce led to a reduction of the national debt.

Frequent protests, though a matter of grave concern, were hardly tantamount to general civil strife. The economy of the Two Sicilies made it the most prosperous state in

Italy. In 1831, the balance of the state's assets was substantial enough to justify a reduction of certain taxes, such as those on flour.

To direct tangible assistance to the poor while instituting safeguards to prevent these funds ending up in the pockets of corrupt bureaucrats, Ferdinand established the Royal Charity Commission.

Ferdinand wed Maria Cristina of Savoy in 1832, the same year he proposed a "League of Italian States," a federalist union that would include the Two Sicilies, the Papal States, Piedmont, Tuscany and Sardinia. This was anathema to the Austrians, Germans and Russians, who saw in it a violation of the terms of the Congress of Vienna and the potential foundation of a new power. Leopold II in Florence seemed indecisive while Carlo Alberto in Turin was evasive, perhaps viewing the proposal as a reflection of Ferdinand's personal ambition to rule the whole of Italy. Reactionary Pope Gregory XVI objected pre-emptively.

In 1838, Ferdinand granted the major part of Sicily's sulfur mining licenses to a French firm. As Sicily provided around eighty percent of the world's sulfur, this did not set well with the British. Indeed, it conditioned Britain's attitude toward Ferdinand over the next two decades.

More immediately, the British threatened a blockade of the Sicilian ports that exported most of the sulfur, along with the confiscation of ships carrying it. In 1840, after a protracted series of diplomatic maneuvers, the British were restored to their former primacy in the market, but much mutual bitterness remained.

Meanwhile, the government sponsored industrial projects that placed the Two Sicilies at the vanguard of the day's technology. This trend saw, for example, the first railway in Italy connecting Naples and Portici in 1839.

Arts, Culture and Science

The arts flourished. Composer Vincenzo Bellini, born in Catania in 1801, was known for his *bravura* works during opera's *bel canto* era. Another Catanian, Giovanni Verga, was a writer of the realist school. His *Cavalleria Rusticana,* later adapted to opera by Pietro Mascagni, was based on events said to have taken place in Vizzini.

Giuseppe Verdi composed *I Vespri Siciliani* about the War of the Vespers. His contemporary, Richard Wagner, composed *Parsifal,* his last opera, during a sojourn in Palermo. In folk art, Sicilian marionettes were inspired by the same medieval culture.

Majolica, tin-glazed earthenware, was already popular in Sicily. Its origins may reach into the island's Aragonese era, perhaps based on a technique introduced by the Arabs.

Sicily had scientists besides the astronomer Giuseppe Piazzi. Stanislao Cannizzaro was a chemist whose work took him to the vanguard of the new field of physics, which he taught at the University of Genoa as "theoretical chemistry." He was one of the first scientists to clearly distinguish between atoms and molecules and define valence. His work led to the development of the periodic table of elements.

By the middle years of the nineteenth century, Sicilian cuisine was well established as a medley of influences formed into a distinctive order. The wines and spirits, the cheeses, the breads, the recipes known today were already popular.

Food was the basis for *sagre* that celebrated local cuisines based on the seasons. Some were harvest festivals. One town might celebrate artichokes, another almonds. Products like ricotta would be celebrated during the spring.

Oenicultural festivals were rare. Sicily's wine country straddles a series of graceful hills between Salemi and Marsala. Following in the footsteps of John Woodhouse, the Inghams and Whitakers greatly increased the scale of Marsala wine production. Until then, the principal crop in this part of Sicily was wheat. Except for Marsala, very few Sicilian wines were produced for sale.

A few entrepreneurs stood out from the crowd. Apart from vintners, one of the first food exporters was the innovative Vincenzo Florio, who sold tuna in jars. In 1840 he signed a partnership with the Inghams, founding a small steamship line.

Every town or quarter had its chief religious festival held on the feast day of the local saint. The festivals of Saint Rosalie (Palermo), Saint Lucy (Siracusa) and Saint Agatha (Catania) were week-long celebrations.

John Goodwin, a British consul who reported on social progress in the Two Sicilies in the years leading up to 1840, was guardedly optimistic about life in the kingdom.

Winds of Change

In 1844 around a hundred armed rioters sympathetic to the ideas of Mazzini were arrested in Cosenza, in Calabria.

The following year, Ferdinand hosted a major scientific congress in Naples. Like similar congresses held in other cities, this one had its political side.

Apart from its excellent commercial relations with Russia, the Two Sicilies negotiated sound trade treaties with Britain, France and the United States.

Throughout Italy, protests were as frequent as ever. Ferdinand used military force to quell a disturbance at Messina in 1847, earning the nickname *Re Bomba,* "King Bomb." Yet he was hardly the only king to use such tactics during this era.

The bomb of popular discontent was not going to be contained, restricted to just one city. In January 1848 it exploded in Palermo.

There were several underlying causes for these protests. A paucity of grain was an obvious catalyst; food shortages and high prices made it easy to enlist the support of the common folk. Europe's "hungry years" of high food prices and an industrial downturn made revolution seem attractive to a new generation.

A new invention, the telegraph, made it easier for the revolutionaries across Europe to communicate. A further impetus in Italy came with electric telegraph lines around Naples in 1852.

In 1856, the Congress of Paris was held to formally end the Crimean War. The Two Sicilies had nothing to do with this but Sardinia-Piedmont did. The Piedmontese representative, Camillo Benso di Cavour, exploited this opportunity to disparage Ferdinand's government in the south. By diplomatic standards, it was an underhanded tactic, especially if one considers that there was no Neapolitan representative present to defend Ferdinand. The same year, the French and the British recalled their ambassadors from Naples.

The next few years saw an effort by external forces to curtail Ferdinand's international influence, but isolating Italy's largest state would not be easy. For now, Ferdinand's detractors in Paris, London and Turin could only await his death, all the while thinking and planning.

Unification

The *Risorgimento,* or "resurgence," was an intellectual movement that began long before the middle years of the nineteenth century. Initially, it was more cultural than political, but before long it was "hijacked" by opportunistic politicians.

Each passing year after the tumultuous revolts of 1848 saw a wider advocacy of Italian unification. Naturally, the greatest support for this came from the political elite of the smaller northern states, who were most likely to benefit from a united Italy. For the most part, this was the aristocracy and the middle class.

Giuseppe Mazzini's anticlerical republican faction was the most "radical" element. Camillo Benso di Cavour led another faction (initially defined as "liberal") which sought to coexist with the established monarchical order; in time, these liberals came to embrace the "moderates" of the bourgeoisie, such as bankers and industrialists, who wanted political continuity but a free- market economy. It was these moderates and liberals, enjoying a certain degree of sympathy from the British, who would plot the course of Italian unification. To that singular end, Cavour was tireless in his backstage machinations.

The role of other forces, such as freemasonry, though real, was never more than peripheral.

Apart from the diminution of Catholic influence in public affairs, the "anticlerical" facet of the unification movement as it manifested itself around 1860 was never quite so liberal or secular as its most vocal apologists subsequently claimed. It certainly was not atheistic, nor much inspired by the Enlightenment.

Although a number of disaffected southerners joined its ranks, the movement's founding leadership was northern; Mazzini was from Genoa, Cavour from Turin. Few of the northerners had spent much time south of Rome. This shaped their views of Italy's southern regions.

Nevertheless, as the movement gained ground, King Ferdinand's cousin in Turin offered him the Crown of Italy if only he would agree to a federalist union, something vaguely conceived along the lines of the Holy Roman Empire and already proposed in 1832. This Ferdinand declined despite his earlier advocacy, explaining that he had no wish to infringe the rights, and the territory, of the Pope, who would never willingly relinquish Rome.

Foreigners, with Britons leading the charge, generally directed their criticism at the Two Sicilies as Italy's largest, wealthiest state, and the one that, at least superficially, seemed to suffer the most from outmoded laws and an entrenched, unenlightened ruling class. These criticisms of an obsolete ethos chained to the Catholic Church were not without merit. However, they must be considered in the context of the times.

Closely allied with the Two Sicilies, the Papal State garnered its share of opprobrium, much of it deserved. The Catholic Church, of course, was a perennial target of Europe's more strident Protestants, but never more so than during the pontificate of sanctimonious Pius IX.

A case could be made that some states in pre-unitary Italy were at least marginally more socially progressive than others. Tuscany first abolished the death penalty in 1786 (only to reinstitute it four years later) and, as we have seen, Piedmont's *Statuto* of 1848 proved to be more enduring than the constitutions enacted in the Two Sicilies, however lofty their aspirations.

In such an environment, it was easy enough to paint the Two Sicilies as being somewhat more repressive than the comparatively "liberal" mini-nations of northern Italy.

But didn't the revolts of 1848 touch Turin as well as Palermo? Wasn't Roman Catholicism the official religion of the "anticlerical" Kingdom of Sardinia? Wasn't the Shroud of Turin venerated just as fervidly as the blood of Saint Januarius in Naples and the bones of Saint Rosalie in Palermo, its provenance equally dubious? Was there not press censorship in Piedmont? Would a recalcitrant journalist in Turin go unpunished if, in his reckless *lèse-majesté,* he wrote an article calling for the deposition of the reigning Savoy?

It would be ridiculous to conclude that life in Sicily was much better than life in Piedmont, but ludicrous to conclude that it was any worse, or that Palermo was in some way backward compared to Turin. There are no precise figures for annual household income outside the aristocracy, but in Sicily proper the *riveli* (tax rolls) provide a general indication of taxation based on familial assets to pay the *donativi*. (Appendix 2 gives figures regarding university enrollment circa 1860, as well as various social and technological achievements before the annexation.)

Sicilian political dissentients went to Piedmont. Where were the Piedmontese dissidents? Where did *they* go?

To America, of course.

The first major wave of Italian immigrants to make their way across the ocean were Piedmontese and Genoans.

While few of these emigrés were political exiles *per se,* it is obvious that they made the long journey to a strange land for a reason. Even if their motivations were purely economic, that begs a number of questions about life in happy, prosperous, democratic "Savoy Land" where, to read the writings of some apologists, everyday existence was one giant, continuous bacchanal of Barolo and Spumante consumed with bresaola, risotto and truffles.

A transitory expatriate was sometime general Giuseppe Garibaldi, a native of Nice (under Savoy rule since 1814) who had fallen out of favor in Turin but would live to play a pivotal role in Italy's unification. Arriving in New York in 1850, he stayed with his friend Antonio Meucci, a Tuscan inventor best known today for his rudimentary experiments in the field of voice transmission via electrical signals over wires.

The truth is that until unification, and indeed for two decades thereafter, the greater part of Italy's emigration came from the regions to the north of Rome, not from the south.

Statistically speaking, the people living in Piedmont, Lombardy, Liguria, Venetia and Tuscany were every bit as impoverished and illiterate as those in Abruzzi, Calabria and Sicily. In rural Piedmont, rice had been planted and harvested the same miserable way for centuries, by women wading through the water, all the while being harassed by the merciless mosquitoes.

Among political theorists, Karl Marx was especially critical of the movement after it transpired because it did not represent, in his view, a step forward. If one were to create a new nation, why a monarchy? Why not a republic like France or even the United States? In the end, Marx was as critical of some of the men who forged the new state as he was of the unitary kingdom they erected upon the embers of the monarchies of the Two Sicilies, Tuscany, Parma and Modena.

While the Two Sicilies didn't need Piedmont, it is clear that Piedmont needed the Two Sicilies, or at least its gold reserves. Based on this measure alone, the wealth of the southern kingdom eclipsed that of all the other Italian states combined, while its national debt was a mere fraction of Piedmont's. This was a matter of public record. Somebody in Turin wanted the gold in Naples. And they were willing to kill for it.

Ferdinand's refusal to accept the Italian Crown left a Savoy as the next logical candidate. For the moment, Ferdinand was an implacable roadblock. He commanded Italy's largest standing army. But redoubtable King Ferdinand wouldn't live forever.

The Undeclared War

Ferdinand II died in May 1859. Francis II, the son of Ferdinand's first wife, saintly Maria Cristina of Savoy, was a very devout young man. That would be his undoing.

The young king lived under the spell of dogmatic, intransigent Pope Pius IX. Zealous Pius was a Pontiff given to pontificating. Too much of it, in fact. Not enough has been written about the influence on Italian unification by the most pertinacious man since 1800 to occupy the See of Saint Peter. If Cavour and his confederates orchestrated the unification, it was Pius IX who provided its instruments, setting the stage for a pathetic performance.

Pope Pius wasn't always opposed to Italian unification; early in his pontificate, during his ephemeral liberal phase, he was willing to accept an Italy united under the Papal tiara. The obvious defect in such a proposal is that no king with any knowledge of history was ever going to accept it!

In Turin, the Savoys knew that their newly-crowned Neapolitan cousin was unlikely to be as ferocious as his father, and they knew something of his piety. Nevertheless, it would be imprudent to risk a major military invasion against a state boasting the largest army on the Italian peninsula. A few zealous Neapolitan generals might actually annihilate a Piedmontese regiment or two. Initially, therefore, support was sought from within the Kingdom of the Two Sicilies. The most efficacious tools were old-fashioned bribery, treason and sedition.

Apart from their more obvious efforts to sow the seeds of sedition among the populace, Piedmontese agents had sought to incite treason among Neapolitan generals for some years, ever since Ferdinand II rejected the Italian Crown.

Likewise, Britain's support for the unification would come in handy. As early as the Plombiéres Agreement of 1858, Cavour was sounding out the French and the British about cooperating in a hypothetical invasion of Sicily he knew Piedmont couldn't achieve on its own.

Yet the Piedmontese ministers didn't want to risk their own troops, and they didn't want to be accused of starting an unprovoked war even though, like other European sovereigns, the Savoys had participated in quite a few. The solution arrived in the person of Giuseppe Garibaldi, a sometime general and occasional mercenary with a checkered past who was willing to fight such a war. Garibaldi had not always enjoyed the good graces of his Savoy masters, but he could be supported tacitly, surreptitiously, and in the event of either a military or diplomatic disaster Cavour could simply deny having ever authorized an attack by a man who didn't even hold an active, formal commission as a Piedmontese general.

Cavour wanted unification but he wanted it on his terms, not Mazzini's, and he was suspicious of Garibaldi.

The first order of business was the occupation of the tiny duchies of Parma and Modena, along with the larger Grand Duchy of Tuscany in early 1860. Here there was little resistance to the overwhelming numerical superiority of the Savoyard forces. Sicily would be left to Garibaldi, with Turin's tacit approval.

In late April, the military command at Messina received news of Garibaldi's impending arrival someplace in Sicily. Further intelligence referred to the transportation of armaments and additional troops, possibly with British logistical support. Acting on these reports and others, Paolo Ruffo, the Lieutenant of the Realm for Sicily, alerted some port officials in the major cities. Cavour ensured that Garibaldi's ships were shadowed along most of the route to Sicily by Piedmontese warships, an "unofficial" military escort.

On May eleventh, Garibaldi's two large vessels landed at Marsala while the commanders of the two British warships stationed there stood by and watched. Indeed, it appears that the British may have actually assisted the landings of the "redshirts" directly, probably by maneuvering into position between them and the Sicilian forces. In the confusion, overpowering Marsala's garrison was not difficult, and naval relief for the Sicilian troops arrived too late to save the day. The city's British wine merchants raised the Union Jack.

Four days later, the garrison at Calatafimi surrendered following token resistance. Several "political" prisoners, mostly aristocrats, were released from the local prison. Here is where wholesale desertion began, swelling the ranks of Garibaldi's army, and other towns fell to the invaders.

Garibaldi's army enlisted more men *en route* to Palermo, where a bloody battle raged in the streets for days. Here the hostilities continued until early June. Traditional unificationist accounts paint the picture of a popular insurrection leading to an "easy" victory over the "cowardly" Sicilian troops who "abandoned" the city. The real pictures, the photographs, tell the story of a highly destructive series of bloody engagements similar to urban guerilla warfare.

The defenders did not lack the courage to fight; what they lacked was courage of conviction. They did not abandon king and country; they were abandoned by generals who failed to act in unison against a common enemy.

Certain details of the Palermo campaign are likely to spark suspicion in the mind of any critical thinker. The events suggest, at the very least, covert planning, if not a wider cast of international players lurking offstage just beyond view. In early April, weeks before Garibaldi's landings, there was an attempted revolt by insurgents, amply supplied with guns and ammunition, at the Gancia monastery. Francesco Crispi, a dissident who later became prime minister, is thought to have masterminded this.

Whether General Ferdinando Lanza's surrender was the result of something other than a looming military defeat is still hotly debated; following a brief truce arranged with Garibaldi on a British ship, Lanza's army resumed fighting for a few days before suddenly capitulating. Less polemical is the fact that in June, following the Battle of Palermo, British ships sent from Malta supplied rifles, and American ships arrived full of arms and northern Italian troops. The war had assumed the character of a multinational invasion bolstered by foreign navies.

Before long, the invading troops were in Calabria making their way north to Naples. Wishing to avoid a civilian slaughter, King Francis II and his wife, Maria Sophia (whose photographs appear in this volume), left the capital in favor of the coastal stronghold at Gaeta to the north. This was a strategic error, and Garibaldi entered Naples in early September. British warships anchored in the Bay of Naples stood by, just in case the invading troops needed assistance.

A series of engagements into early October made it clear that there were still people willing to defend the realm.

Nevertheless, the war was lost. The Savoys got Sicily and the British obtained their sulfur.

Elections and Insurrections

A plebiscite held in the invasion's aftermath confirmed Savoy rule with an astounding ninety-nine percent of eligible Sicilian voters favorable to the new regime. Were this a legitimate balloting, its results would be studied around the world as a rare electoral phenomenon, for how many free elections are ever won with such a majority?

The numbers tell the story. The only eligible voters were literate males of at least twenty-five years of age who declared a certain taxable income, a tiny fraction of the adult male population considering a general literacy rate of (at best) twenty percent.

The "official" result is 432,053 votes favorable to annexation and a mere 667 in opposition, in a general population (including men under twenty-five, women and children) estimated at approximately 2,232,000. Moreover, the figure reported (equal to some twenty-five percent of the *total* adult population, including men under twenty-five years of age *not* entitled to vote) suggests a far higher level of literacy and taxable personal income than there actually was, rendering voting by any more than 300,000 literate, taxable men over the age of twenty-five mathematically impossible.

Throughout Italy, region after region confirmed the annexation in referenda resulting in majorities invariably comparable to that claimed for Sicily.

In the wake of the lost war, a number of military officers who had loyally fought against the Piedmontese invasion in mainland Italy, particularly around Gaeta, found themselves incarcerated, along with numerous partisans — often branded as "brigands" by the new government — who continued an armed resistance in the countryside. A few were Sicilians, though most were from Naples and such regions as Calabria and Basilicata. Fenestrelle, an Alpine fortress converted into a prison, thus became Italy's first concentration camp in 1862, eventually housing some three hundred political prisoners. In most cases, their only "crime" was to have supported the crown and country they were sworn to defend. Others, tried as "war criminals" by the new regime, were pardoned or received suspended sentences.

Before long, a series of "extraordinary" taxes were levied on the residents of the former Two Sicilies to defray the cost of the undeclared war, the invasion, of 1860-1861. The treasury, holding more gold than what was held by all the other pre-unitary states combined, had already been pillaged.

The Rothschilds were forced to close their bank in Naples in 1863 in view of the precipitous decline in the economy following the annexation.

An anti-Savoy, pro-Bourbon revolt broke out in Palermo in September 1866. Leading to martial law and suppression by Piedmontese troops, the riots prompted many in Turin to question how such a protest was possible in view of the Savoys' phenomenally high "approval rating" a few years earlier.

Life in the New State

In 1867, most church property was confiscated, including many monastic estates. This was catastrophic because the schools operated by the religious orders had been the chief means of educating young children, and there were no public (state) schools to replace them.

Compulsory public instruction for children in primary grades was instituted in 1877, but very few public schools were built in Sicily before 1900. The first state schools established by this law opened in Tuscany, Piedmont and other regions north of Rome.

The school history texts were propagandistic. Sicily's every shortcoming was starkly highlighted while none of Piedmont's were even mentioned. A glaring omission was the infamous Piedmont Easter Massacre, mentioned earlier, which saw some 1700 Waldensians slaughtered by Savoyard troops in 1655, followed by another bloody suppression in 1686.

In 1882 the first deep sulfur mines opened in Sicily. These were tunnels and shafts, as opposed to the open-pit "strip" mines that had been used previously. Too often, children were pressed into labor as miners because few adults were skinny enough to get through the narrow passages. What resulted can only be described as slavery, but the government made little effort to prevent it. Philip Carroll, the United States Consul in Palermo, was expelled from Italy in 1890 for exposing these inhumane conditions in a published report.

Italians

The surfeit of Italy's grandiose political propaganda did nothing to change reality.

By this time, most Italians were virtually destitute. Until now, most Italian emigration was from the north, not the south.

Francesco Crispi, a bigamist, became Italy's first Sicilian prime minister in 1887, but this did not help his fellow Sicilians. In 1894, during his second term in office, the *Fasci Siciliani,* a rural workers' movement, was brutally suppressed, resulting in lengthy prison sentences for the leaders.

The Crispi government fell when Italian forces were defeated at Adwa, in Ethiopia, in 1896 during an ill-fated imperialist campaign. The thrashing of Italian troops led the nation's army to be ridiculed internationally for generations.

In early May 1898, a series of mass protests broke out around the country over the scarcity and high price of bread amidst what was rapidly becoming a full-fledged famine. Even before the food shortages, many Italians lived in conditions bordering on debt peonage. In Milan, over a hundred demonstrators were killed by the army in the infamous Bava-Beccaris Massacre.

The ever-present propaganda was ridiculously transparent. "Outside elements" were a frequent scapegoat. Born and raised in Tuscany, and then resident in the United States for just six years, anarchist Gaetano Bresci, who assassinated King Umberto I in retribution for the carnage that took place in Milan, was portrayed as "an American," as if New Jersey were a breeding ground for regicidists.

The New Century

Rome responded inadequately to the catastrophic earthquake at Messina in 1908, the first major natural disaster to confront the Kingdom of Italy and an event that revealed the country's woeful state.

The lives of the common people were still miserable. Following a visit in 1910, Booker T. Washington, an American born into slavery, wrote that, "the condition of the colored farmer in the most backward parts of the southern states in America, even where he has the least education and the least encouragement, is incomparably better than the condition and opportunities of the agricultural population in Sicily."

With the dismemberment of the Ottoman Empire, Italy occupied Libya in 1911. This is where the nation's worst war crimes began, as indiscriminate massacres in small villages. As the Ottomans retreated, the Italians also seized the island of Rhodes. Like its domestic policy, Italy's imperial policy was based on ineptitude.

Although Italy found herself on the winning side in the First World War, which she entered belatedly in 1915, the cost in Italian lives was high. A disproportionate number of draftees were from the South; many northerners obtained exemptions by working in factories built in the North, often with government support, while the South languished in poverty.

Trench warfare on the Austrian front found Carabinieri snipers a hundred meters behind the Italian lines, posted there to shoot deserters.

South Tyrol was formally, and legally, annexed to Italy in 1920, with the Istrian peninsula annexed less legally four years later. By that time, Italy was governed by a new regime.

Fascist Italy

Benito Mussolini's Fascists were placed in power by King Victor Emmanuel III in 1922, and by the time of the Giacomo Matteotti murder two years later the nation was well on its way to becoming a nasty dictatorship. If most Italians were oblivious to the transition, it was only because the Kingdom of Italy, with its press censorship and repression of labor movements, already seemed like a police state.

During this trying period Sicily produced some of Italy's best writers; the poet Salvatore Quasimodo and the playwright Luigi Pirandello come to mind. The latter was an unrepentant Fascist. Vitaliano Brancati, on the other hand, came to despise the regime.

Only rarely was scientific achievement recognized, with Fascist sympathizers like Secondo Campini and Guglielmo Marconi being the favored exceptions.

Sicilian-born Giovanni Gentile, Fascism's chief ideologist, oversaw publication of the nationalist *Enciclopedia Italiana.*

"Those who can make you believe absurdities," said Voltaire, "can make you commit atrocities." That is precisely what happened in Italy.

The depravity of Fascism is well-known. What is less widely known is that the invasion of Ethiopia of 1936 led to Italy becoming the first nation to acknowledge committing crimes against humanity (in addition to generic war crimes), and that Italy eventually had to pay war reparations to that nation as well as Albania, Greece and the Soviet Union (Russia).

In 1937, the year that Italy resigned from the League of Nations, physicist Emilio Segrè, working under primitive conditions at the University of Palermo, discovered the first "artificial" element, technetium (Tc). One of Segrè's colleagues was Ettore Majorana, a gifted young Sicilian whose sophisticated body of work included insightful theories on neutrino masses nearly a century before this became a popular line of research. Recognizing Majorana's landbreaking theories regarding electrons and positrons, important in nuclear fission and chain reactions (principles governing the function of nuclear power reactors and the first atomic bombs), Enrico Fermi praised him as a genius. Majorana disappeared in suspicious circumstances in 1938.

The anti-Semitic laws of 1938 were particularly distasteful, if not altogether surprising in a dystopia that now sought to emulate Nazi Germany.

Elvira Mancuso, of Caltanissetta, was an educator and writer, and the most famous of just a few Sicilian feminist activists in an era that viewed as anathema the notion of gender equality. Censored and silenced by the Fascist regime, she lived to see its demise, and the subsequent emergence of something approaching equal rights for Italy's women. Maria Messina followed in her footsteps.

Fascism prompted the departure of the best and the brightest: Enrico Fermi, Arturo Toscanini, Maria Montessori, Emilio Segrè, Umberto Nobile.

The Second World War

Italy's invasion of Greece and the Balkans was a comedy of errors requiring German military support to bolster the inept Italian forces. Fascist attempts to bomb Malta into oblivion could not compensate for the Italians' lack of radar, which left warships susceptible to nocturnal destruction by Britain's Royal Navy. El Alamein was a debacle that saw the Italians routed by the British.

Allied victories in North Africa paved the way for the invasion of southern Europe. The Allied military operations bore bluntly descriptive names like Mincemeat, Corkscrew and Husky which few Italians could comprehend, the teaching of English having been outlawed by the regime.

The war arrived in Sicily on a February morning in 1943 when the first shells fell upon Palermo's Magione district, killing nearly a hundred civilians. In a subsequent raid a single massive bomb collapsed an underground air-raid shelter in the square behind the apse of Palermo Cathedral, killing two hundred.

Following this extensive "carpet bombing" of Palermo as well as Messina, the Allies landed in Sicily in the summer of 1943. The ensuing campaign proved highly destructive, with historical treasures like the Norman castle at Troina all but obliterated in protracted fighting between Americans and Germans.

Alfredo Guzzoni, the general charged with defending the island, fled with his troops across the Strait of Messina, abandoning a piece of Italy. By then, most Sicilian Fascists were already burning their black shirts and party membership cards. Cut off from the party hierarchy, they had to think for themselves, some for the first time in their lives.

Nationalism died a rapid death. At Licata, local women on balconies launched rubbish onto the heads of Italian prisoners marched down the town's streets by the Americans.

Led by Bernard Montgomery and George Patton, the Allies had won the day, and the century. Italy was emasculated, *quod erat demonstrandum.*

For their part, the occupiers were shocked at the abject poverty, the ubiquitous squalor, that confronted them on the conquered island. Despite having been forewarned of these realities, many were surprised that most homes lacked plumbing and electricity. Telephones and refrigerators were virtually unknown. Fleas and disease were everywhere. Illiteracy was rife. Ten percent of the population held seventy percent of the wealth. Women were little more than chattel.

It fell within the purview of the occupiers to feed the Sicilians. Having inherited a mediocre administration from the Italians, the occupation government had to contend with acute food shortages and every other kind of emergency. For the first time, the Sicilians had access to drugs to cure malaria.

In September 1943, capricious King Victor Emmanuel III announced Italy's armistice with the Allies and soon abandoned Rome.

In Palermo, Stefania Mantegna, who was something of an anti-Fascist, hosted a ball for local aristocrats and American military officers at her sumptuous home, Palazzo Gangi. In this land of contrasts, a street a few blocks away became the scene for a much more desperate spectacle.

The Allies had left day-to-day police duties to the Italians. In October 1944, these Fascist-trained troops fired into a crowd of Palermitans protesting for food, killing twenty-four and wounding over a hundred in the *Strage del Pane,* the Palermo Bread Massacre. It was an eerie reprise of the Milan massacre of 1898.

In 1945, the Germans surrendered officially to the Allied Command headquartered at Caserta, the Bourbons' palace outside Naples. The Italian Campaign had cost fifty thousand Allied lives.

In June 1946, the month following King Umberto's concession of Sicilian autonomy, a referendum, which saw Italian women vote for the first time, ousted the monarchy and exiled the royal family. Although there were irregularities in the balloting, this referendum was not nearly so outlandish as the plebiscite of 1860.

Not Plato's Republic

Control of the nascent republic was ceded to the Italians with the Paris Peace Treaty of 1947. With this document, Italy guaranteed freedom of the press and freedom of religion to those living in the country. A new constitution was enacted in 1948.

War crimes trials were avoided because, in a divided country, the Americans and British did not wish to open the door to leftist movements that might drive Italy to an alliance with the Soviet Union. Thousands of Italian troops taken prisoner in the failed invasion of Russia were repatriated only in 1955, the same year Italy was permitted to enter the United Nations.

Very little about Fascism or the lost war was taught to Italian school children in succeeding generations. Even today, most Italians born after 1950 know virtually nothing about the country's misadventures in Ethiopia.

For a few years, Italy was buoyed by American largesse in the form of the Marshall Plan and other programs. By 1960, the Italian economy had begun to improve, helped along by the same mass emigration that had always acted as a "safety valve" in the overpopulated nation.

Italy became part of NATO, and an American naval air station was established near Catania.

During the Cold War, it was considered expedient to prevent Italy, with its endemic political unrest, from moving too far to the left. Despite an occasional "great compromise" with the opposition, the conservative Christian Democrats would control the country for decades. In Sicily, where they were invariably the vast majority, they made pacts with the Mafia to ensure support from what, after Lazio and Lombardy, was the country's most populated region.

Patriotism is tenuous at best. For every book celebrating the sesquicentennial of Italy's unification in 2011 there was another challenging the "official" version of it that for more than a century had disparaged everybody south of Rome. Commemorative festivities were largely ignored.

The Mafia

Rooted in the rustic banditry of the last years of the eighteenth century and nourished by Sicilians' distrust of authority, this form of criminality evolved to become ubiquitous. Extortion and narcotics were its hallmarks, but it permeated every part of the Sicilian economy. Only the demise of the Christian Democrats, and a series of specific laws, facilitated serious attempts to restrict the worst activities of the Mafia. Public awareness has played a role in this.

Until around 1800, organized crime, such as it was, consisted principally of banditry and the corruption of the estate agents, the infamous *gabellotti,* who controlled the larger *latifondi* on behalf of absentee landlords who preferred to live in the major cities. Despite some fanciful theories, and generic use of the word *mafia* before that time, there is little evidence of this form of criminality flourishing before 1780, but extortion was commonplace by 1900.

In Italy, criminality of this kind (such as the Camorra in Naples) was often dismissed as part of the secretive mentality that permeated life in the south. In the United States, it was regarded as a form of gangsterism.

Although the Mafia was never as centralized as some would have us believe, meetings of its leaders, the "Cupola" in Palermo and the "Commission" in Apalachin (New York), in 1957, lent it a greater hierarchal structure and made it a truly international enterprise. Early public revelations came from Leopoldo Franchetti in Italy in 1876, and Joseph Valachi in the United States in 1963.

In 1925, Cesare Mori, the "Iron Prefect," arrived in Sicily to quell the Mafia. This had mixed results. Unfortunately, Mori's frequent solution, which was typical of the regime he served, was to jail every suspect he could find, sometimes without so much as the benefit of a show trial. This practice later permitted actual *mafiosi* to present themselves to the invading Americans as victims of Fascism.

That the Americans enlisted the cooperation of *mafiosi* like Calogero Vizzini during the Allied occupation following Operation Husky (in 1943), and even placed a few in positions of minor authority (as mayors of small cities), has given rise to some popular myths.

Deported to Sicily following the war, Sicilian-born Charles "Lucky" Luciano helped the American government to obtain the cooperation of longshore (port) workers in New York following the fire that destroyed the SS Normandie (an ocean liner being retrofitted for troop transport) in February 1942; Nazi sabotage was suspected in the destruction of a vessel believed to be faster than any German submarine. Luciano was not involved directly in Operation Husky, although he provided some intelligence.

Much has been made of the fact that the American mobster Vito Genovese, who knew Calogero Vizzini and Lucky Luciano, served as an interpreter during the occupation. In fact, Charles Poletti, the former governor of New York who became the United States Army's chief administrator for public affairs in Sicily, had no social connection with these men; as he was fluent in Italian, Poletti would not need a translator.

The idea that the American military would be incapable of fighting its way from Gela to Palermo without Mafia help is patently absurd. There is little doubt, however, that Vizzini, Luciano and Genovese advanced their criminal careers through their activities in Italy immediately after the war.

By 1960, the Sicilian Mafia was imitating American gangsterism. The phrase *cosa nostra* ("our thing") is, in fact, an Americanism.

The effects of Mafia influence are ubiquitous. After 1950, the organization constructed much of Palermo and Catania, with disastrous results in terms of urban planning (or the lack of it). Most of the mayors and senators friendly to the organization were Christian Democrats; until the 1980s it was rare for a candidate of any other party to get elected to an important position.

The Mafia's growth was facilitated by the failure of juridical authorities in either country to recognize the organization as a reality until the 1970s, when it was selling heroin.

Finally, in 1987, some *mafiosi* were sentenced in the "Maxiprocesso," the first major trial of Sicilian organized crime figures in Italy under new laws, coinciding with the "Pizza Connection" trial in the United States.

That did not eradicate the Sicilian organization or stop the killing, and Palermo's airport is named after two judges assassinated by the Mafia in 1992 (the authors of this book heard the blast of the bomb that killed Judge Paolo Borsellino). The following year, the Mafia killed a parish priest, Giuseppe Puglisi, in the Brancaccio district of Palermo. In 2011, a former governor of the Sicilian Region was sent to prison for having corroborated with the Mafia.

The concept of the "Mafia· family" is an import from America; in Sicily the organization was traditionally based more on localized cells, the *cosche* (clans) of specific towns or urban districts, than on strictly hereditary lines.

Extortion, though less commonplace than in the past, remains a mainstay of organized crime. In fact, the Chinese merchants of Palermo and Catania pay "protection money" to two criminal organizations, the one from China and the one in Sicily.

The twenty-first century has found Mafia money invested in mainstream businesses such as supermarkets and other stores. Government contracts in fields like construction still fall into the hands of the Mafia, which also controls part of Sicily's water supply. The Mafia's corruption of the public sector now touches the left as well as the right.

Mafiosi used to be secretive; now their names and mugshots are routinely published in the *Giornale di Sicilia*. Disorganized crime.

Corruption

Efforts to combat the modern Mafia, though largely successful, have met with resistance because Italian organized crime is a symptom of underlying problems rooted in clannishness, clientelism, nepotism, *raccomandazioni* (undeserved preferments) and corruption, endemic phenomena that are not always illegal or even socially unacceptable in Italy. They are the order of the day.

Appointments to professorships, for example, often go to the children, spouses, friends or lovers of tenured professors. (Indeed, the lack of meritocracy in academia and industry prompts much emigration, and has led to an Italian "brain drain.")

In 2015, the politically-appointed director of Palermo's chamber of commerce, a public agency that administers business licensing and other services, admitted demanding a payoff of a hundred thousand euros to grant an exclusive concession to a pastry maker for shop space at the local airport. The man was exposed when his victim wore a cell phone "wire" during their meeting while police were listening at the other end. Although this was not a Mafia-related offense (the director was acting on his own and simply "needed the money"), it was fostered by a bizarre social environment where payoffs of this kind are considered normal. Indeed, such incidents are usually accepted by Italians as part of an "Italian way of life."

It should be noted that such things are fairly commonplace throughout Italy, not only in the south.

Wholesale corruption will finally be eliminated when Italian society itself is reformed. It will take time, but the process has begun.

The New Multiculturalism

A growing number of immigrants from Asia and Africa now live in Italy, especially in the larger cities. In Sicily, they populate parts of Catania and especially Palermo, which have become, in a sense, multicultural again after seven centuries.

A generation from now, the children of these immigrants will make up a significant fraction of the Italian population, perhaps something approaching twenty percent.

In Palermo there are now several mosques and, for the first time in five centuries, a synagogue near the site of the one that was closed in 1493.

The immigrants have been received in Sicily with far less racism and bigotry than in the regions north of Rome. This is hospitality in the grand tradition of King Roger II.

4
GENERAL HISTORY

As the previous chapter indicates, Sicily's history is lengthy and sometimes complex. Very few works approach our island's three millennia in great detail or with a great degree of accuracy.

There is no universal paradigm of what constitutes the "perfect" history or the "best" historian. In its most essential form, a history, be its orientation political or social, need only present events, developments and details accurately, with some sense of chronology. Even a distinctive voice, an occasional analysis or a thematic perspective, though highly desirable, is not absolutely necessary in every case. A clear prose style is an advantage, naturally, but the greatest distinction among historians is simply that the better historian, like the better surgeon, teacher or engineer, *knows* more.

The books mentioned in this chapter were written by people who have studied Sicilian history for some years, rather than by authors who "just decided to write a book about Sicily." While we might occasionally question their emphasis or approach, and perhaps even their conclusions, we would never, in three thousand years, doubt the knowledge or expertise of the historians whose work is recommended. As you will see in successive chapters, some of these authors have written other books as well as those mentioned here. Their work speaks for itself.

What makes these authors experts?

Expertise in historical studies is not just a matter of academic credentials, though one would hope that somebody who has earned an advanced degree would not fall prey to the kind of errors that plague the work of the novice. It is based on a keen knowledge of a subject and careful application of the historical method.

It isn't just a job. The best historians have a true passion for their subject that transcends a passing familiarity. However, they should not be "obsessed" to the point of identifying with it too closely to be objective. Historians who lose their sense of reality have been known to cultivate a monopolistic, quasi-territorial jealousy, leading to the poor treatment of anybody who trespasses on their turf by daring to publish something on the same topic. This occurs when, for example, a historian wishes to be identified as the *only* expert on a certain place, period or personage (a typical effect of this being the overzealous criticism of the work of colleagues viewed as "rivals").

The historians whose generalist histories of Sicily are mentioned here have consulted original "primary" sources like the *Bibliotheca Historica* of Diodorus Siculus written in antiquity, or the *Chronicon* of Romuald of Salerno (the title page of our favorite print edition is shown at the end of this chapter) written in the twelfth century, rather than relying exclusively on the "secondary" work of scholars like Thomas Fazello, whose post-incunable *De Rebus Siculis* (1558) was the first printed history of Sicily. For the benefit of anglophone students who are not proficient in Latin, a few scholars, like Graham Loud, Gwenyth Hood and this book's two authors, have translated *entire* medieval chronicles for publication.

For further insight into the way history is (or should be) written, we highly recommend Barbara Tuchman's timeless *Practicing History,* first published in 1981. For now, let's direct our attention to Sicilian history.

Sicily in General

A very good choice, when it is available in reprint or reissue, is *A History of Sicily* by Moses Finley (1912-1986) and Denis Mack Smith (1920-2017). This was published in three volumes in 1968 and, for the most part, it has withstood the test of time.

The first volume, *Ancient Sicily to the Arab Conquest,* was authored by Professor Finley, one of the most insightful historians to ever specialize in ancient Greece and Rome. (For an interesting summary of his groundbreaking theories and work, see *M. I. Finley: An Ancient Historian and his Impact,* published in 2016.) The second volume, *Medieval Sicily 800-1713,* was written by Denis Mack Smith, who also wrote the third volume, *Modern Sicily after 1713.*

A distinguished specialist in Italian Studies, Professor Smith was known for challenging the platitudes that tainted Italian history as it was presented between 1860 and 1945, something that earned him the ire of ageing unificationists and Fascists even as his books were translated for publication in Italy.

We are reluctant to suggest that students obtain three volumes to study Sicily, and you may be tempted to use the shorter version of this work. Although the condensed, single-volume edition of 1986 may suffice for some needs, it is not generally recommended. It is far too superficial for most students' interests, barely touching the ancient and medieval periods, and virtually ignoring the Arabs. In considering the Second World War, it reflects the ill-informed opinion espoused by the book's third author, a younger scholar who did the editing, that the Mafia is largely the fruit of fantasy (something stated on page 214). Any future editions of the book will lack the exclusive stamp of the three authors, all now deceased.

A more practical suggestion than the condensed edition of *A History of Sicily* is the recent survey by John Julius Norwich, an eloquent popularizer whose work is very accessible. This informative volume was published in 2015 in Britain as *Sicily: A Short History from the Ancient Greeks to Cosa Nostra* and in the United States with the slightly more palatable title *Sicily: An Island at the Crossroads of History.* It is a fine overview.

The few reservations here are that the book treats certain historical clichés with less than the critical rigor they deserve, and it does not always reflect the most recent research in the field. For example, the author ascribes a certain credibility to the referendum of 1860, which gave the new regime ninety-nine percent of the votes (see Chapter 3 for our simple statistical analysis).

Lord Norwich's book might be more effective if used in tandem with Denis Mack Smith's *Italy and Its Monarchy,* published in 1989.

Another choice is Louis Mendola's book, *The Kingdom of Sicily 1130-1860* which, despite its title, actually covers Sicilian history from antiquity to 1950. This presupposes a supplementary work for the period after 1950 or for more detail on, for example, the ancient Greeks or the Second World War.

None of these books is perfect, and none should be taken as gospel. It should, as ever, be remembered that history is not religion. In the study of history there are experts but no infallible authorities. Facts do not become facts simply because they are published and believed.

Works dedicated more specifically to ancient, medieval or modern Sicily are considered in the next chapters.

Beyond Sicily

Depending on the focus of your course, it may be appropriate to include a text that considers Sicily in the broader context of Mediterranean history. Perhaps the course you are teaching is dedicated to the Mediterranean generally, and not to Sicily exclusively.

Here there are two excellent entries by true Siculophiles, *The Great Sea: A Human History of the Mediterranean* (2011) by David Abulafia and *The Middle Sea: A History of the Mediterranean* (2006) by John Julius Norwich. We suggest that you read both before choosing one over the other.

For a history of Italy to place Sicily in context, an exceptionally competent exposition that transcends tired tropes is *The Pursuit of Italy: A History of a Land, its Regions and Their Peoples* (2011) by David Gilmour.

Hybrid History

A hybrid genre of works comprises what are essentially "guides" containing a fair amount of historical information. Consisting chiefly of essays reflecting their authors' commentary based not only on historical facts but descriptions, experiences and impressions (along with the occasional interview), these books cannot take the place of the histories described above for use as course texts or for a student in search of general information. In fairness, it must be stated that they do not purport to be pure history texts, yet they do offer the reader far more than will be found in a tourism guide that includes restaurant and hotel information.

These books are reminiscent of the diaries and letters written by Europeans like Patrick Brydone and Johann Wolfgang von Goethe who visited Sicily during a "grand tour" in the eighteenth century. Published in London in 1838, *The Normans in Sicily,* by Henry Gally Knight, was the first modern "historical travelogue" in English dedicated to Norman Sicily.

By Jeremy Dummett is *Palermo, City of Kings* (2015) and *Syracuse, City of Legends* (2010). Another fine entry is Joseph Farrell's *Sicily: A Cultural History* (2012). To this elite list must be added John Keahey's *Seeking Sicily* (2011).

Our only criticism of books in this "history and travelogue" category, be their geographic focus Italy or Ireland or China, is that they occasionally present views at variance with current academic research or include the kind of statements that can mislead a student. The genre is influenced as much by memoirs and travel writing as solid history. However, this kind of book is engaging, affording the casual reader a glimpse of a place lengthier than what one finds in a travel article and less demanding than a history. One commends their fresh "outsider's view" but, as we stated earlier, the great majority of historical works published about Sicily in English are written by foreigners anyway.

This emerging "hybrid history" genre may represent the future of much that is published in the field of general-interest (mass market or "popular") history, and anecdotes even made their way into Lord Norwich's history of Sicily, mentioned above. This narrative style seems to be what most readers and publishers want. These books are not necessarily part of any movement (e.g. postmodernism); they are a trend.

CHRONICON
ROMUALDI II.
ARCHIEPISCOPI SALERNITANI.
In Chriſti nomine incipit Chronica.

DE ÆTATIBUS.

Rima mundi ætas eſt ab Adam uſque ad diluvium, côtinens annos, juxtaHebraicam veritatem mille ſexcentos quinquaginta ſex, juxta ſeptuaginta verò Interpretes duo millia ducentos quadraginta duos ; generationes verò juxta utramque editionem numero decem , quæ univerſali eſt deleta diluvio , ſicut primam cujuſque hominis oblivio deinergere conſuevit ætatem . Fuerunt Noë filii tres , ex quibus ita. ſunt ortæ gentes . De Japhet quindecim . De Cham triginta . De Sem XXVII. Sem annos duos poſt diluvium genuit Salem : à quo Samaritæ & Indi . Sale genuit Heber : à quo Hebræi . Heber genuit Falech , cujus tempore turris ædificatur , & linguarum diviſio fit . In ſolo Heber priſca remanſit lingua , quia in ea conſpiratione non fuit . Turris verò duo millia CLXXIV. dicitur paſſuum . Hanc Nembroth gigas conſtruxit . Hac ætate Scitharum regnum oritur , ubi primus regnavit Ihannus . Tunc & regnum Ægyptiorum ubi primus regnavit Thoes . Dehinc regnum Aſſiriorum , ubi primus regnavit Belus , quem dicunt Saturnum quidam : deinde Ninus , qui condidit

A| Ninivem . Hoc tempore Abraham naſcitur : & poſt mortem Nini à Semiramide Regina reædificata eſt Babylonia , ubi regnavit annos quadraginta .

Secunda ætas à Noë uſque ad Abraham generationes juxta Hebraicam veritatem complexa decem , annos autem ducentos nonaginta duos ; porrò juxta ſeptuaginta Interpretes anni MLXXII. Generationes verò XI. hæc verò quaſi pueritia fuit generationis populi Dei , & ideo in lingua inventa eſt Hebræa , à pueritia namque homo incipit noſcere loqui, quæ idcirco appellata eſt , quòd fari non poteſt . Ab Adam itaque uſque ad Abraham juxta Hebraicam veritatem computantur anni mille nongenti quadraginta octo , ſecundùm ſeptuaginta Interpretes fiunt anni tria millia trecenti quatuordecim .

Tertia ab Abraham uſque ad David generationes juxta utramque auctoritatem XIV. annos verò, ſecundùm Hebræorum auctoritatem nongentos quadraginta duos complectens; juxta ſeptuaginta verò Interpretes anni tria millia CXXXVII. hæc velut quædam adoleſcentia fuit populi Dei , à qua ætate incipit homo poſſe generare , propterea Matthæus Evangeliſta generationum ab Abraham ſumpſit exordium , qui etiam pater multarum gentium conſtitutus eſt , quando mutatum nomen accepit . Ab Adam verò juxta Hebræorum auctoritatem uſque ad David fiunt anni duo millia octingenti nonaginta , ſecundùm ſeptuaginta Interpretes tria millia CV. Cur autem annorum hæc diverſitas ſit , in ſequentibus oſtendetur .

Quarta à David uſque ad tranſmigrationem

R₃-

Early edition of the chronicle of Romuald of Salerno, 1725

F.THOMÆ.FAZELLI.
SICVLI.OR.PRÆDICA/
TORVM.

DE REBVS SICVLIS DECADES DVAE, NVNC
PRIMVM IN LVCEM EDITAE.

HIS ACCESSIT TOTIVS OPERIS IN-
DEX LOCVPLETISSIMVS.

CAVTVM EST PHILIPPI ANGLIAE, HISPANIAE,
Siciliæq; Regis,Pauli. IIII. Pont. Max. ac Venetæ Reip.priuilegio,ne
cui has Decades de Siculis rebus ad decennium in eorum di-
tione vel imprimere , vel alibi impreſſas venales
habere , neue in ſermonē Italicū iniuſ-
ſu authoris vertere ſub mul
ſta liceat .

First published history of Sicily, by Thomas Fazello, in 1558

128

5

ANCIENT HISTORY AND ARCHEOLOGY

"If you wish to understand anything," said Aristotle, "observe its beginning and its development." Sicily was important enough in the world known to the Greeks, Punics and Romans that her ancient history is rarely studied on its own, as if Sicily were identified with a specific ethnicity. Indeed, one cannot speak of a true Sicilian identity until the Middle Ages (that's fodder for our next chapter).

This presents a challenge to the study of ancient Sicily in that it may necessitate several texts instead of just two. One can expect no less in considering the history of a large island in the middle of the Mediterranean.

Although the earliest historians, such as Diodorus Siculus, Timaeus, and Thucydides, should not be ignored (and are available in translation), the emphasis here is the wider context of ancient Sicilian history viewed from a modern perspective. Some historical information may be discerned in the work of early poets like Theocritus.

An obvious recommendation is Moses Finley's *Ancient Sicily to the Arab Conquest,* mentioned in the previous chapter. It could be argued that some of his work has been overshadowed by recent research, but in fact most of it is still valid. Although the Victorian age saw Edward Freeman writing about Sicily, much of his work has been eclipsed by recent discoveries.

Not to be overlooked is Robert Leighton's *Sicily Before History: An Archeological Survey from the Paleolithic to the Iron Age* (1999). Salvatore Piccolo's *Ancient Stones: The Prehistoric Dolmens of Sicily* (2013) is a concise study of its subject.

For an emphasis on sites, a fine entry is *The Archaeology of Ancient Sicily* by Ross Holloway (1991). Here Jeremy Dummett's book on Syracuse (see the previous chapter) is also useful, though obviously localized.

For an idea of what some sites looked like millennia ago, a complementary work is *Ancient Sicily: Monuments Past and Present* (2006) by Gaetano Messineo and Emanuela Borgia.

Greek Sicily

There are numerous specialized works. Erik Sjoqvist's *Sicily and the Greeks* (1973) concentrates on the Greek colonization of regions controlled by the Sicanians, Sikelians and Elymians. Another work with a specific emphasis is *Archaic and Classical Greek Sicily: A Social and Economic History* (2016) by Franco De Angelis.

Sicily: Art and Invention between Greece and Rome (2013), by Claire Lyons, Michael Bennett and Clemente Marconi, reflects the work of numerous scholars. Its focus is the period from the Battle of Hymera in 480 BC (BCE) to the fall of Syracuse to Roman forces in 212 BC. First published by the J. Paul Getty Museum in connection with an exhibit, this anthology features beautiful photographs. Another interesting, richly-illustrated volume published by the Getty Museum is *The Greek Cities of Magna Graecia and Sicily* (2006), by Luca Cerchiai and Lorena Jannelli.

Malcom Bell's *Morgantina Studies* (1981) is a fine contribution to the field.

The Peloponnesian War (2004 edition), by Donald Kagan, approaches its subject with great erudition. Another fine resource is *The Landmark Thucydides* (1998), Robert Strassler's updated, annotated edition of the classical work.

A good overview of linguistic realities is *Language and Linguistic Contact in Ancient Sicily* (2012), an anthology of papers edited by Olga Tribulato.

Punic Civilization

For a breezy introduction, consider Sanford Holst's *Phoenician Secrets* (2011), for something on the more scholarly side Josephine Quinn's *In Search of the Phoenicians* (2017).

A good outline of Carthaginian history, though very little of it deals with Sicily specifically, is *The Carthaginians* (2010) by Dexter Hoyos.

There is no dearth of books on the Punic Wars. Here the difficulty is selecting one. A good overview is *Carthage Must Be Destroyed: The Rise and Fall of an Ancient Civilization* (2012) by Richard Miles. Adrian Goldsworthy brings us *The Punic Wars* (2001). Slightly less lengthy is *The Punic Wars: Rome, Carthage and the Struggle for the Mediterranean* (2005) by Nigel Bagnall.

Roman Sicily

Not to be overlooked are classical "source" works like Livy's history of Rome, *Ab Urbe Condita,* available in various editions.

Very little among modern works tends to focus explicitly on Sicily as a Roman province, a status the island endured over a very long period. There is no defined canon.

This has led less astute authors to concoct the ridiculous notion that "very little happened in Roman Sicily." Nothing could be further from the truth. The fact is that, as an important part of Rome's empire, the cities of Sicily, though prosperous, did not enjoy the political independence they did under the Carthaginians and Greeks, nor the prestige that would come with the Arabs and Normans.

A seminal work on sites and details is Roger Wilson's *Sicily Under the Roman Empire: The Archaeology of a Roman Province* (1990).

A good academic anthology to complement this is *Sicily from Aeneas to Augustus* (2000), edited by Christopher Smith and John Serrati.

Mythology

Who are the Sicilians of myth? To mention just a few, Persephone gathered flowers in the Vale of Enna, Arethusa emerged as a spring in Ortygia, Hephaestus and the Cyclops ruled the fiery summit of Etna, Scylla and Charybdis challenged Odysseus, the nymph Kyane swam in the river that bears her name, and Aeolus was the Keeper of the Winds.

That is the short list. Temples to Greek deities abound in Sicily.

Some Sicilians known through mythology are quasi-legendary. King Kokalos of the Sicanians welcomed a grieving Daedalus to Sicily following the death of Icarus, the boy who flew too high.

A good compendium of Greek mythology is *The Greek Myths* (1955) by Robert Graves (now available in a single volume as "The Complete and Definitive Edition"), but some readers may find Edith Hamilton's *Mythology* (1940) more engaging.

Here an interesting entry is Karl Galinsky's *Aeneas, Sicily and Rome* (1969).

6
MEDIEVAL HISTORY

The "Middle Ages" are usually dated from the fall of the Western Roman Empire in the fifth century until the fall of Constantinople and the Byzantine Empire in the fifteenth.

Although Denis Mack Smith's *Medieval Sicily 800-1713* does a reasonably thorough job of covering a broad period, some of the books mentioned here better address specific ones.

The last three decades have seen a greater quantity and quality of scholarly work published in English about Sicily's Middle Ages, and particularly the Norman era, than about any other period of our island's history. For the most part, the result has been beneficial for those studying this subject.

Some of the books in this chapter, like the last one, are anthologies, edited collections of academic papers that, in certain cases, were first presented at conferences. (This kind of publication was mentioned in Chapter 1.) Informative as some of these publications may be, many carry a high price tag, perhaps more than a hundred dollars or pounds for a book running to four hundred pages, because the publishers must make a profit from short press runs and just a handful of purchasers, principally university libraries. In selecting such material, or suggesting it to students (or perhaps recommending it for purchase by your institution's library), it is good to bear in mind that some of these papers, even a few that seem quite specialized, are far less original than they purport to be. One need not dwell on this, but we have observed that, pressured to produce original work, some scholars have resorted to extremely esoteric, indeed pedantic, inquiry into recondite topics which have, in fact, already been studied at length.

An anthology of the kind we are describing is *A Companion to Medieval Palermo.* Published in 2013 with a list price of 187 euros (220 US dollars), it consists of sixteen papers of widely varying quality, and only a few that present anything like original scholarship or insight. The editor's stated objective was to publish the papers of some professors whose work was not previously available in English. Noble as that intention may be, the result was an expensive volume that, with the exception of a few chapters by distinguished scholars like Henri Bresc and Annliese Nef, is useful mostly as an introduction. Under most circumstances, it is unrealistic to expect students to buy such a book, and even some librarians are reluctant to do so. For comparison, consider that Cambridge University Press released a book of similar length, *The Latin Church in Norman Italy,* by Graham Loud, a scholar whose work never disappoints, for about half that price, with paperback and electronic editions available for far less.

Some dissertations that make their way into book form are based on tenuous ideas and questionable theses.

Fortunately, some academic papers can be downloaded from the internet at little or no cost.

Despite our misgivings about certain publications, some work, like the translations and analyses of primary resources, is useful and even elucidating, and here a post-medieval example comes to mind. Following a war that ended in 1504, Spain took control of the Kingdom of Naples from the

French. After five centuries, deciphering the unique code used by King Ferdinand of Aragon to communicate with Gonzalo de Cordoba during the Italian campaign was a significant achievement.

Except for the books mentioned in Chapter 4, very few works survey the medieval history of Sicily in anything like a general way. Most of the books currently available reflect studies of specific periods. Overviews like *The Peoples of Sicily* examine the Middle Ages more widely than some works, but if you seek a reasonably profound study, then you are likely to end up considering books that deal with particular periods or reigns. Fortunately, these exist.

Works relating to the Byzantines and Arabs concern not only specific periods of Sicilian rule by these peoples but the *civilizations* of these cultures, which flourished in Sicily into the thirteenth century.

The Goths and Vandals in Sicily

Very little has been written about the brief Gothic and Vandalic rule of Sicily. However, some informative books consider these peoples more generally, and more sympathetically than past writers were inclined to do.

One of these is *People and Identity in Ostrogothic Italy, 489-554* (1997) by Patrick Amory, and another is *The Vandals* (2010) by Andrew Merrills and Richard Miles.

Byzantine Greek Sicily

If we consider that Greek was spoken in some localities of the Kingdom of Sicily into the Swabian era during the thirteenth century, and that icons and other Byzantine art (discussed later) remained popular during this period, it is clear that this influence lasted for a long time. Here, however, we encounter the same phenomenon we found in the last chapter with Roman Sicily, where the island was part of a broader civilization and culture. A rather similar situation exists with the Fatimid era although, as we shall see, there are more books about the Arabs in Sicily than the Byzantines.

The best survey is *Byzantine Sicily: Greek and Orthodox Civilization in the Middle Ages* (2018) by Lorenzo Casati and Christopher Seal, both theologians.

For the background of Byzantine culture generally, the seminal work in English is Steven Runciman's *Byzantine Civilisation* (1969). Runciman himself, who one of this book's authors knew, was a remarkable scholar and an interesting character. Like Moses Finley, he is the subject of a biography; this is Minoo Dinshaw's *Outlandish Knight: The Byzantine Life of Steven Runciman,* published in 2017.

Byzantium (1995), the three-volume series by John Julius Norwich, makes for a fine introduction. A condensed version of this is *A Short History of Byzantium* (1998).

The *Alexiad* was first translated for publication in English by Elizabeth Dawes in 1928. A good modern translation is Edgar Robert Ashton Sewter's annotated work, *The Alexiad of Anna Comnena,* published by Penguin in 1969.

Judith Herrin's *Byzantium: The Surprising Life of a Medieval Empire* (2009) is a fine addition to the field. Another is Barbara Hill's *Imperial Women in Byzantium 1025-1204: Power, Patronage and Ideology* (1999).

An interesting document is to be found in "Foundation of a Monastery in Byzantine Calabria 1053/54" a translation by Adele Cilento and David Routt, in *Medieval Italy: Texts in Translation* (2009).

Ernst Kitzinger wrote books dealing with the Byzantine mosaics of Norman Sicily. A fine example of his work is "The Mosaics of the Cappella Palatina in Palermo," in *Art Bulletin,* number 31 (New York 1949).

The Mosaics of Norman Sicily (1950), by Otto Demus, is another excellent entry.

Muslim-Arab Sicily

Like Byzantine Greek culture, the Aghlabid, Kalbid and Fatimid influence lasted in Sicily into the thirteenth century.

The best introductory overview of the Muslims and Arabs in Sicily published thus far is *A History of Islamic Sicily* (1975, 2000), by Aziz Ahmad. It is presently out of print.

A useful resource is Ronald Broadhurst's eloquent translation of *The Travels of Ibn Jubayr* (1952).

Jeremy Johns' *Arabic Administration in Norman Sicily: The Royal Diwan* (2002) is a fine study. He also wrote "The Norman Kings of Sicily and the Fatimid Caliphate," in *Anglo-Norman Studies XV* (1995).

Another good exposition is Julie Anne Taylor's *Muslims in Medieval Italy: The Colony at Lucera* (2005).

Alexander Metcalfe's *Muslims and Christians in Norman Sicily: Arabic Speakers and the End of Islam* (2011) is an insightful study into a specific period, with clues to the Arabic influence on the Sicilian language. By the same author is the more general work *The Muslims of Medieval Italy* (2009), which covers the status of the Muslims until 1300.

A History of Muslim Sicily (2011), by Leonard Chiarelli, is also useful.

"The Islamic Origins of the Common Law," *North Carolina Law Review*, volume 77, number 5 (June 1999), by John Makdisi, is a landmark exposition.

"The Jews in Sicily under Muslim Rule in the Light of Geniza Documents," in *Italia Judaica 1* (1983), by Gil Moshe, is a fine study.

Another interesting study is "Ibn-Hawqal, the Cheque, and Awdaghost," *Journal of African History,* volume 9, number 2 (Cambridge 1968), by Nehemia Levtzion.

More generally, one may wish to consider *The Fatimid Empire* (2017), by Michael Brett.

A useful resource in translation is *The Chronicle of Ibn al-Athir for the Crusading Period from al-Kamil fi'l-Ta'rikh, Part 2, 541-589/1146-1193* (2007), by Donald Richards.

Norman Sicily

A fine survey is *The Norman Kingdom of Sicily* (1992) by Donald Matthew. To complement this is Hubert Houben's *Roger II of Sicily* (2002). Two books by Jacqueline Alio present biographies of Sicilian queens during this period, namely *Margaret, Queen of Sicily* (2016) and *Queens of Sicily 1061-1266* (2018). Joanna, the queen consort of William II of Sicily, is considered in *The Daughters of Henry II and Eleanor of Aquitaine* (2014) by Colette Bowie.

John Julius Norwich wrote two fine books, *The Normans in the South* (1967) and *The Kingdom in the Sun 1130-1194* (1970). The only criticism of these is that some of the information presented (such as the anachronistic nickname of Walter "of the Mill") has been corrected by subsequent research.

For background, Barbara Kreutz's *Before the Normans: Southern Italy in the Ninth and Tenth Centuries* (1996) addresses the Lombard-Byzantine rule of peninsular Italy.

The Eastern Schism: A Study of the Papacy and the Eastern Churches during the XIth and XIIth Centuries (1955), by Steven Runciman, offers a good consideration of its subject. On a theological note, this may be complemented by John Meyendorff's *Orthodoxy and Catholicity* (1966).

A series of fine essays by various scholars is presented in *The Society of Norman Italy* (2002).

An insightful economic study was penned by the erudite David Abulafia, namely *The Two Italies: Economic Relations Between the Norman Kingdom of Sicily and the Northern Communes* (1977).

To complement the work of Kitzinger mentioned under "Byzantine Greek Sicily," a good choice is *The Cultures of His Kingdom: Roger II and the Cappella Palatina of Palermo* (1997) by William Tronzo.

We cannot mention every specialized study, but an example is "The Attempted Byzantine Alliance with the Sicilian Norman Kingdom 1166-1167," in *Papers of the British School at Rome* (London 1956) by John Parker.

On an ecclesiastical level are *Latin Monasticism in Norman Sicily* (1938) by Lynn Townsend White and *The Latin Church in Norman Sicily* (2007) by Graham Loud.

Also by Graham Loud is *Roger II and the Creation of the Kingdom of Sicily* (2012), which brings us translations of several important chronicles and the Assizes of Ariano and, with the late Thomas Wiedemann, *The History of the Tyrants of Sicily by Hugo Falcandus* (1999), which includes part of the *Chronicon* of Romuald of Salerno.

An insightful essay is Donald Matthew's "The Chronicle of Romuald of Salerno" in *The Writing of History in the Middle Ages: Essays Presented to Richard William Southern* (Oxford 1981).

Hugh Falcandus still sparks lively debate centuries after his death. Gwenyth Hood's "Falcandus and Fulcaudus Epistola ad Petrum Liber de Regno Sicilie: Literary Form and Author's Identity," in *Studi Medievali,* 3rd Series, XL (June 1999) is one of the most sober studies. Its thesis contrasts with that of the distinguished Evelyn Jamison's A*dmiral Eugenius of Sicily: His Life and Work and Authorship of the Epistola ad Petrum and the Historia Hugonis Falcandi Siculi* (1957).

The History of the Normans by Amatus of Montecassino (2004) is an excellent translation by Prescott Dunbar.

Kenneth Wolf wrote *Making History: The Normans and Their Historians in Eleventh-century Italy* (1995). He authored a translation of Godfrey (Geoffrey) Malaterra's chronicle, published as *The Deeds of Count Roger of Sicily and of His Brother Duke*

Robert Guiscard (2005). Graham Loud's monograph *The Age of Robert Guiscard* (2002) deals with the Hautevilles' incursions into Apulia, Calabria and Sicily.

The Administration of the Norman Kingdom of Sicily (1993), by Hiroshi Takayama, is a fine study.

Another insightful study is "The Crown and the Economy under Roger II and his Successors," in *Dumbarton Oaks Papers,* number 37 (Washington 1983), by David Abulafia.

"The Daughter of Al-Andalus: Interrelations between Norman Sicily and the Muslim West," *Al-Masaq: Journal of the Medieval Mediterranean,* volume 25, issue 1 (London 2013), by Lev Kapitaikin, is a good analysis.

A fine biography of the Staufen who cast a shadow over Europe is John Freed's *Frederick Barbarossa: The Prince and the Myth* (2016).

Swabian Sicily

Written in verse, the chronicle of Peter of Eboli covers the reign of Henry VI and his consort, the Sicilian heiress Constance. Here a fine translation is Gwenyth Hood's *Book in Honor of Augustus* (2012). Richard of San Germano (see below) also considered this period.

Not surprisingly, the focus of most of the books dealing with the Swabian era is Frederick II. Although *Frederick the Second* (1931), by Ernst Kantorowicz, was the best known until recently, its point of view, and even some of its sources (which may be forgeries) must sometimes be questioned. A better choice might be *The Emperor Frederick II, Immutator Mundi* (1972) by Thomas Curtis van Cleve. For a more accessible biography from a rational point of view, we suggest *Frederick II: A Medieval Emperor* (1992) by David Abulafia.

The Liber Augustalis or Constitutions of Melfi (1971), by James Powell, is a translation of this legal code with notes.

William Tronzo's *Intellectual Life at the Court of Frederick II Hohenstaufen* (1994) brings us a cultural overview.

To complement this are several books (also mentioned in the chapter on the Sicilian language) which consider the Sicilian School of poetry. Foremost among these is *The Poetry of the Sicilian School* (1986) by Frede Jensen. A more recent entry, which considers works in Arabic as well as Middle Sicilian, is *The Kingdom of Sicily 1100-1250: A Literary History* (2005) by Karla Mallette. A fine translation of the *Contrasto* of Ciullo of Alcamo, a supreme example of romantic court poetry, appears in Jacqueline Alio's *Queens of Sicily* (2018) accompanied by the original Sicilian text.

An informative book about the Papacy during the early years of Swabian rule is *Innocent III: Leader of Europe 1198-1216* (1994) by Jane Sayers. See also James Powell's *Innocent III: Vicar of Christ or Lord of the World?* (1963).

Two chronicles survive that were written in the Kingdom of Sicily during the reign of Frederick II. *The Chronicle of Richard of San Germano* (2002) was translated by Graham Loud. *The Ferraris Chronicle* (2017) is a translation by Jacqueline Alio.

The only English biography of the son of Frederick who reigned until 1266 is Louis Mendola's *Manfred of Hohenstaufen, King of Sicily* (2018). A supplementary work is the same author's translation of the chronicle that recounts the reigns of Frederick's sons; this is *Frederick, Conrad and Manfred of Hohenstaufen, Kings of Sicily: The Chronicle of Nicholas of Jamsilla* (2016).

A number of supplementary works may be useful, for example Bjorn Weiler's *Henry III of England and the Staufen Empire 1216-1272* (2006) and George Coulton's *From St Francis to Dante: Translations from the Chronicle of the Franciscan Salimbene 1221-1288* (1907).

Angevin and Aragonese Sicily

The greatest modern account of the events from the Battle of Benevento to the War of the Vespers is *The Sicilian Vespers: A History of the Mediterranean World in the Later Thirteenth Century* (1958) by Steven Runciman.

Translations by Louis Mendola appear in *The Battle of Benevento according to Andrew of Hungary and Saba Malaspina* (2018).

King Charles I of Naples remains a contentious figure. A departure from the usual demonization of him is to be found in Jean Dunbabin's *Charles I of Anjou: Power, Kingship and State-Making in Thirteenth-Century Europe* (1998).

Sicily's Rebellion against King Charles: The Story of the Sicilian Vespers (2015) is Louis Mendola's translation of the memoir of John of Procida.

A fine treatment of court life, with an eye to the human element, is Nancy Goldstone's *Four Queens: The Provençal Sisters Who Ruled Europe* (2007).

Insightful accounts and analyses of Sicilian history during the long Aragonese era will be found in *An Island for Itself: Economic Development and Social Change in Late Medieval Sicily* (2003) by Stephan Epstein, and *The Decline and Fall of Medieval Sicily: Politics, Religion and Economy in the Reign of Frederick III, 1296-1337* (1995) by Clifford Backman.

The Crusades

The Crusades, of course, were undertaken over the course of a long era, and Messina was a springboard for most of them. A good primer is *The First Crusade and the Idea of Crusading* (1986) by Jonathan Riley-Smith, while a fine overview is *A History of the Crusades* (1951) by Steven Runciman.

James Reston's *Warriors of God: Richard the Lionheart and Saladin in the Third Crusade* (2002) is a good treatment. Another recommendation, with an emphasis on crusading orders like the Hospitallers and Templars, is *The Monks of War: The Military Religious Orders* (1996), by Desmond Seward.

The Jews

Studies of the Jews of Sicily tend to emphasize the Middle Ages. For Benjamin of Tudela, see *The Itinerary of Benjamin of Tudela* (1907), a translation and commentary by Marcus Nathan Adler. *The Itinerary of Rabbi Benjamin of Tudela* (1840), by Adolf Asher, is also useful; this includes a Hebrew text so eloquently simple that teachers of the language use it with beginning students.

Another traditional source that mentions Sicily is Obadiah of Bertinoro, quoted in *Miscellany of Hebrew Literature* (1872).

Shlomo Simonsohn's *Between Scylla and Charybdis: The Jews in Sicily* (2011) is a condensed version of extensive studies that consider Judaism in Sicily *in toto*.

Complementary to this is *The Former Jews of this Kingdom: Sicilian Converts After the Expulsion 1492-1516* (2003) by Nadia Zeldes.

A charter of 1171 in Latin and Greek consulted by Jacqueline Alio during research for the first biography of Queen Margaret of Sicily

7

MODERN HISTORY

Bearing in mind that both were written before 1970, and therefore cannot reflect the wealth of research undertaken since then, Denis Mack Smith's books *Medieval Sicily 800-1713* and *Modern Sicily after 1713* have much to offer.

Louis Mendola's history, *The Kingdom of Sicily* (2015), presents a fair amount of information to 1950. John Julius Norwich's *Sicily* (2015) also covers the period.

That having been said, any serious survey of modern Sicily will include other works as well. This may focus on, among other things, the island as part of the Spanish Empire, occasionally the Austrian Empire, and then the united Italy.

1500-1700

An interesting figure was the Holy Roman Emperor Charles V, who ruled during the sixteenth century and visited Sicily. A very concise entry suitable to the needs of students more interested in Sicily than the monarch's many other dominions is *The Reign of Charles V* (2004) by William Maltby. For a more detailed biography, there is Harald Kleinschmidt's *Charles V: The World Emperor* (2004).

A sub-topic is the Knights Hospitaller, to whom Charles granted Malta as a fief. A fine introduction is Desmond Seward's *Monks of War* (1996).

An interesting study is *The Government of Sicily under Philip II of Spain: A Study in the Practice of Empire* (1951) by Helmut Koenigsberger. Philip II died in 1598.

1700-1920

Here the era framed by the years 1700 and 1920 is more convenient than conceptual, as what is presented in some of these works reaches beyond 1920 and into the middle of the twentieth century.

The Bourbons of Naples (1956) and *The Last Bourbons of Naples* (1961), by Harold Acton, are an excellent treatment of the era from 1700 to 1860. Angus Campbell's *Sicily and the Enlightenment: The World of Domenico Caracciolo, Thinker and Reformer* (2016) augments this.

The Force of Destiny: A History of Italy Since 1796 (2008), by Christopher Duggan, is a good overview of how the united Italy came to be. A fine complement to this is Robert Putnam's *Making Democracy Work: Civic Traditions in Modern Italy* (1993).

Denis Mack Smith's *Italy and Its Monarchy* (1989) is the most accurate general history (in any language) of Italy's monarchy and its institutions after 1860, the unification period. *The Fall of the House of Savoy* (1972), by Robert Katz, is a highly critical, sometimes sardonic, look at the dynasty that ruled a tenuously-united Italy until 1946, with insightful sections on the unification movement of 1860 and its aftermath.

The Pursuit of Italy: A History of a Land, Its Regions, and Their Peoples (2011), by David Gilmour, is a sober, objective view of Italy and a regionalism based on centuries of history.

Lucy Riall brings us several insightful titles. *Sicily and the Unification of Italy: Liberal Policy and Local Power 1859-1866*

(1998) is one of the better books written about this period. *Garibaldi: Invention of a Hero* (2008) is a pragmatic examination of the controversial life and fragile cult of the man infamously described by Karl Marx as King Victor Emmanuel's "taxi driver." *Under the Volcano: Revolution in a Sicilian Town* (2013) is an erudite analysis of life in a small Sicilian locality during the nineteenth century, and the execution of local civilians by Garibaldi's invading troops in 1860.

John Dickie brings us *Darkest Italy: The Nation and Stereotypes of the Mezzogiorno 1860-1900* (1999), a highly informative work that describes the origin of the *divario* (division) between Italy's north and south following unification.

In much the same way that Soviet historians uttered nary a word against the Russian Revolution, Italians writing between 1860 and 1960 sought to defend the unification movement and even, in some notorious cases, Italy's disastrous choices involving Fascism and the Second World War. Sadly, this is also true of some Italians writing today. Anybody considering works in translation that were first authored by Italians should bear in mind that these may be extremely biased, perhaps presenting information that is simply inaccurate.

A number of papers and articles published in English in 1909 and 1910 reported the Messina earthquake of 1908 and the government's ineptitude in responding to it.

The Man Farthest Down: A Record of Observation and Study in Europe (1912), by Booker T. Washington, has several chapters dedicated to the plight of rural Sicilians and their living conditions in 1910. Nothing like this was published in Italy during the same period. Indeed, as we have seen, an American consul was expelled from Italy for reporting such conditions twenty years earlier.

Fascism

In most respects, this subject is presented far more accurately by historians raised abroad than by those educated here in Italy.

Looking first at the effects of Fascist policy beyond Italy's shores, *The Addis Ababa Massacre: Italy's National Shame* (2017), by Ian Campbell, presents a series of facts unknown to the overwhelming majority of Italians. Robert Katz's book (mentioned in the previous section) also addresses such genocide. Ali Muhammad as Salabi's *Omar al Mokhtar: Lion of the Desert* (2011) examines the Sanussi movement against the Italian occupation of Libya; as we mentioned in Chapter 1, a film about this subject was effectively banned from public screening in Italy until 2009.

Very few books published in English deal with Fascism in Sicily specifically, but it behoves students to understand the nature of the beast. An excellent overview is A *History of Fascism, 1914-1945* (1995) by Stanley Payne. An examination of Fascist origins and ideology is to be found in *The Anatomy of Fascism* (2005) by Robert Paxton.

A fine reference is Philip Cannistraro's *Historical Dictionary of Fascist Italy* (1985). Roy Palmer Domenico's *Italian Fascists on Trial* (1991) is a good exposition.

Italians' writings about Fascism are often tainted by strong political bias emanating from the far right or (occasionally) the far left, and should be approached critically.

The Second World War

The chief works on the Second World War in Sicily are *Bitter Victory: The Battle for Sicily 1943* (1988), by Carlo d'Este, and *The Day of Battle: The War in Sicily and Italy 1943-1945* (2007), by Rick Atkinson.

The Battle of Sicily: How the Allies Lost Their Chance for Total Victory (1991), by Samuel Mitcham and Friedrich von Stauffenberg, is an analytical work with keen insights into Axis strategy and the Allied response.

Operation Mincemeat: The true spy story that changed the course of World War II (2010) is Ben Macintyre's bestselling book about the fascinating espionage operation and intrigue that led to what was then (until the Normandy Invasion) the world's largest amphibious military invasion. One of its planners was a young Ian Fleming. Another informative read about what took place behind the scenes is *The Luciano Project: The Secret Wartime Collaboration of the Mafia and the US Navy* (1977) by Rodney Campbell; see also Tim Newark's book in the next chapter.

The official United States military history is available online as Andrew Birtle's *World War II Campaigns: Sicily,* published by the U.S. Army Center of Military History (CMH Pub 72-16).

Soft Underbelly (1968), by Trumbull Higgins, also deals with Sicily. *Operation Husky: The Allied Invasion of Sicily* (1977), by Stanley Pack, is a solid military history.

William Breuer's *Drop Zone Sicily* (1983) is a more personal account. Samuel Eliot Morison's *Sicily-Salerno-Anzio* (1954) is a good history written in a time before "political correctness." *The Italian Campaign* (1987), by John Strawson, offers a good account of the campaign generally.

Also recommended is Mark Zuehlke's *Operation Husky: The Canadian Invasion of Sicily* (2008).

An interesting resource is *A Travel Guide to World War II Sites in Italy: Museums, Monuments and Battlegrounds* (2010) by Anne Leslie Saunders.

Those who study this subject extensively in Italy will encounter the pseudo-scholarship of "historians" who are, in effect, Fascist apologists. Most of the revisionism concentrates on two areas. Firstly, it attempts to depict Italian soldiers as being more competent, patriotic, disciplined or motivated than most actually were. Secondly, it seeks to paint isolated incidents of Americans shooting civilians and prisoners (most notably in the infamous "Biscari Massacre") as part of a "cover-up." This "conspiracy theory" is antithetical because these tragic cases were always known, the records of the incidents (initiated by Captain John Compton and Sergeant Horace West) being readily accessible in American archives, and even reported in Carlo d'Este's book, as well as American documentaries aired on television. Conversely, the Italians' torture and shooting of civilians in Greece and the Balkans (and other occupied territories) was part of an official policy of repression and reprisal, and the perpetrators went unpunished, with a few enjoying successful political careers in post-war Italy; indeed, very little about the war is taught in Italian schools and few Sicilians even know that there is a Canadian war cemetery at Agira.

Sicily in the Italian Republic

Danilo Dolci's *Sicilian Lives* (1981), a work in translation, recounts the experiences and observations of a social activist who arrived in Sicily in 1952 and undertook a ceaseless war against corruption and the Mafia.

Peter Robb's *Midnight in Sicily* (1998), though not a formal history in the true sense (parts of it read like a memoir), considers the demise of Italy's "First Republic" and its corruption, its connections with the Mafia, and other complexities of Italian life. See also Alexander Stille's *Excellent Cadavers* (in the next chapter).

Pino Aprile's *Terroni: All that has been done to ensure that the Italians of the South became southerners* (2011) is a kind of updating of the period covered by John Dickie's *Darkest Italy*.

History of Autonomous Sicily 1947-2001 (2002), by Romolo Menighetti and Franco Nicastro, is a work in translation that explains the political organization of Sicily's regional assembly and its authority.

Gender studies, genealogy and the Mafia are considered in the next chapter.

8

SPECIAL TOPICS

A number of specialized topics constitute popular and academic non-fiction studies and genres. Three are considered
here.

Women's Studies

Jacqueline Alio's *Women of Sicily: Saints, Queens and Rebels*
(2014) is the only book in English to focus on this aspect of
gender studies from a socio-historical perspective, although it
is not an academic study.

Giacomo Pilati's *Sicilian Women: True Stories of Conviction and
Courage* (2008), a work in translation, presents profiles of four-
teen contemporary Sicilian women through interviews, some
worthier of more attention than others.

Another entry is Margaret Chapman's *Milocca: A Sicilian Village* (1928). Published belatedly in 1971, this is considered the
first anthropological study of rural Sicily by a qualified scholar
from outside Italy. It generally confirms the perspectives about
Sicilian women expressed by writers like Maria Messina.

Linda Reeder's *Widows in White: Migration and the Transforma-
tion of Rural Italian Women, Sicily 1880-1920* (2003) is based on

case studies and statistical research. It is a useful point of reference for social context during this period. The first chapter begins with an accurate description of rural Sicilian life in the town of Sutera.

Jane Hilowitz's *Economic Development and Social Change in Sicily* (1976) is a study of the Siracusa area from the beginning of the twentieth century to the 1970s, and the role of women is considered at length.

Renate Siebert's *Secrets of Life and Death: Women and the Mafia* (1996) deals specifically with women in the Mafia's long shadow, both victims and participants.

Few scholarly studies relating to women's issues emanate from Sicily. One that saw the light of day is "The Family, Honour and Gender in Sicily: Models and New Research," by Ida Fazio, published in November 2004 in *Modern Italy* 9(2). Another interesting study is Bernard Cook's "Sicilian Women Peasants in the Nineteenth Century," published in 1997 in *Consortium on Revolutionary Europe 1750-1850: Selected Papers.*

Queens and queenship comprise a specialized sub-field. For the Middle Ages, two biographical works that focus on Sicily are Jacqueline Alio's *Margaret, Queen of Sicily* (2016) and *Queens of Sicily 1061-1266* (2018). *The Daughters of Henry II and Eleanor of Aquitaine* (2014), by Colette Bowie, considers Joanna Plantagenet, the queen consort of William II of Sicily.

An interesting entry is *The Diary of Queen Maria Carolina of Naples 1781-1785: New Evidence of Queenship at Court* (2017) by Cinzia Recca.

Genealogy

Presently, only one book deals exclusively with Sicilian genealogical research. We submit for your consideration Louis Mendola's aptly-titled *Sicilian Genealogy and Heraldry* (2013). In addition to a consideration of family history and armorial heraldry (coats of arms), it outlines the history and ranks of the Sicilian nobility.

There are various books and websites dedicated, more generally, to Italian genealogical research that mention Sicilian records.

The Mafia

A plethora of books populate what has become a genre, but a few stand out.

John Dickie has written two books on the Mafia. *Cosa Nostra: A History of the Sicilian Mafia* (2004) is, as its title implies, a general history. The focus of *Mafia Republic: Italy's Criminal Curse* (2013) is the Mafia's connection to Italian politics.

Peter Robb's *Midnight in Sicily* (mentioned in the last chapter) also considers the influence of the Mafia in Italian politics, as does Alexander Stille's *Excellent Cadavers* (1996).

One of the finest works ever written on this subject is *Octopus: The Long Reach of the International Sicilian Mafia* (1990) by Claire Sterling. A largely ignored, underrated book that describes the connections between the Sicilian and American mafias is Ralph Blumenthal's *Last Days of the Sicilians* (1988). Both of these publications may be considered outdated in certain respects.

Historical views based on investigations in specific localities are provided by Anton Blok in *The Mafia of a Sicilian Village 1860-1960* (1975), and by Peter and Jane Schneider in *Reversible Destiny: Mafia, Antimafia and the Struggle for Palermo* (2003).

There are also biographies of deceased *mafiosi*.

Tim Newark's *Mafia Allies: The True Story of America's Secret Alliance with the Mob in World War II* (2007), based partly on recently-declassified records, approaches its subject very astutely. An earlier entry was Rodney Campbell's book *The Luciano Project* (1977), mentioned in the last chapter. *The Mafia and the Allies:*

Sicily 1943 and the Return of the Mafia (2007), by Ezio Costanzo, is a work in translation that reflects a somewhat narrower focus than Newark's book; like many Italian authors' works on the war and the Mafia, it is rather politicized and therefore not extremely objective.

Letizia Battaglia: Passion, Justice, Freedom (1999) is a collection of photographs with a focus on Mafia victims by a Sicilian photojournalist.

The Vine Whisperer (2017), which Count Filippo Testa co-wrote with Susannah Elliott, tells the story of a Sicilian vintner whose business is threatened by the Mafia.

It should be noted that Mafia and anti-Mafia "industries" flourish in Sicily. Among the former are such things as "god-father tours" for fans of Francis Coppola's movies about an American Mafia family. Promoting visits of locations where scenes in these movies were filmed, these excursions arguably may be oriented more toward cinematic history than overt glorification of the Mafia. Unfortunately, it is sometimes difficult to distinguish one from the other.

On the opposite side of the coin are certain anti-Mafia organizations that promote their own books, tours and lectures, sometimes implying themselves to be "the only Sicilians opposed to the Mafia." This risks leaving the visitor with the ridiculous impression that most Sicilians are somehow connected to organized crime.

9
SICILIAN LANGUAGE

Sicilian is the Romance language that emerged by 1200 after the Normans latinized Sicily. Despite what you may occasionally read, there is no evidence of the use of this vernacular language, usually classified as "Italo-Dalmation," before the end of the Norman era.

Into the first decades of the twelfth century, most Sicilians spoke Greek, Arabic or both. Chroniclers identified them by the languages they spoke. Referring to the plight of Roger Hauteville and his wife, Judith, when besieged at Troina during an unusually cold winter in the first phase of the conquest of Sicily, Godfrey Malaterra states that, *Graeci vero et Sarraceni, quibus omnis patria favens pro libito patebat, plurima replebantur abundantia.* "Instead, the Greeks and Saracens received provisions from the entire region and were supplied abundantly."

A good study of the medieval Sicilian dialect of Arabic, which survives in a modern form as Maltese, is *Siculo Arabic* (1996) by Dionisius Agius.

Influenced chiefly by Latin but to some degree by Greek, Arabic, Provençal, German and Norman French, the new Romance tongue, which was spoken in parts of Calabria and Puglia as well as Sicily, formed the foundation for the Sicilian

School of poetry that flourished at the court of Frederick II. The lengthiest poem in this language to survive until our times is the *Dialogue,* or *Contrasto,* of Ciullo of Alcamo, although the only extant text of that work is somewhat tuscanized.

Its importance, if not its eloquence, was recognized by Dante in his *De Vulgari Eloquentia* ("On Eloquence in the Vernacular") written early in the fourteenth century, where he quotes a line from Ciullo's poem:

Et dicimus quod, si vulgare sicilianum accipere volumus secundum quod prodit a terrigenis mediocribus, ex ore quorum iudicium eliciendum videtur, prelationis honore minime dignum est, quia non sine quodam tempore profertur, ut puta ibi: "Tragemi de'ste focora, se t'este a boluntate."

An excerpt from Ciullo's poem:

Rosa fresca aulentissima chi apparj inver la state, le donne ti disirano pulzelle et maritate; trajimi di'ste focora, si de'ste a boluntate; per te non aviu abbento notte e dia, penzando pur di vuy, madonna mia.

A close translation:

"Rose fragrant and fresh that blooms in summer, maids and maidens envy you; deliver me from this raging flame. For you I have only restless days and nights, thinking always of you, my lady."

Middle Sicilian enjoys a special place in the study of the history of the Crown of Aragon, a thalassocracy (shown in one of this book's maps) that included Sicily after 1282. Sir Steven Runciman, the polyglot scholar who wrote the first major English work on the War of the Vespers, read Middle Sicilian proficiently.

The language brings us passages like this one from the memoir of John of Procida, written around 1290:

Livausi Misser Palmerj Abbati, e dissi, "Signuri re laudatu sia Dea, chi ben esti vinutu e ffactu nostru intendimentu per vostra bontati e quilla di Misser Iohannj di Prochita. Inperò vi plaza di quista cosa aja bon mezu e bonu finj, sì comu à avutu bonu incomenzamentu. Ma ben vurria kj vuj fussivu vinutu cum pluj genti, chi si lu Re Carlu dixindi per tucta la ysola di Sichilia, lu quali avi ben quindichi milia hominj a ccavallu, sì kj nui avirimu troppu a ffarj a ccumbactirj cum ipsu. Et inperò mj pari kj penzamu di avirj pluj agentj di quali parti avirj si'ndj putissi, inperò eu cryu kj Missina sia perduta, tantu era ristricta et in succaru di vidanda."

Which is to say:

There Lord Palmeri Abbati rose to speak. "Sire," he said, "God be praised that you and John of Procida, in your goodness, have acceded to our request for assistance. We hope that this enterprise proceeds and then ends as well as it has begun. But I wish that you had brought a larger army. King Charles can call upon as many as fifteen thousand mounted men if he launches a full attack against Sicily. It will be all we can do just to meet him on the field of battle. So it seems to me that we will need more men, I know not from where. Anyway, I believe Messina to be lost, being besieged nearly to the point of starvation."

The page of the *Spinelli Codex* from which this passage was translated appears at the end of this chapter.

An important distinction is drawn between Middle Sicilian (sometimes *Old* or *Medieval* Sicilian), the tongue written and spoken into the fourteenth century, and Modern Sicilian, or simply *Sicilian,* the language spoken today. Modern Sicilian was influenced by Catalan, Neapolitan and localized usages. To the ear, the Catalan spoken in Barcelona sounds much like the Sicilian spoken in Palermo.

It should be noted that there are actually several dialects of this modern language; for example, the Sicilian spoken in some towns in the Nebrodian Mountains bears vestigial traces of the tongue spoken by the "Lombards" of southern peninsular Italy who arrived with the Normans.

Contrary to a belief propagated outside Italy, Sicilian is not yet a "dead" language. Indeed, it is probably the most widely spoken second language in Italy. For a few older Sicilians, it is a first language.

At some time after 1400, in view of its literary use by poets like Dante, Tuscan supplanted languages like Sicilian and Neapolitan among the ever-diminishing literate classes. This tongue evolved into "Italian."

A result of this development was that, compared to Tuscan, Sicilian was thenceforth written rather rarely, and it came to be identified with the less literate social classes that eventually comprised the majority of the population. Thomas Fazello's monumental history of Sicily, mentioned earlier, first appeared in Latin, but it was later published in Italian, not Sicilian.

After 1860, Italian unification, and then the Fascist regime, provided a further impetus to discouraging Italy's various vernacular languages. Sicilian was unjustifiably disparaged as a lowly "dialect" of Italian even though the oldest narrative prose written in one of the Italian languages (and quoted earlier) was composed before 1300, not in Tuscan or Umbrian but Middle Sicilian.

Traditionally, the ruling classes necessarily spoke at least some Sicilian in order to communicate with everybody else, and as recently as the earliest years of the nineteenth century we find occasional traces of it in legal documents like the *riveli* (tax rolls) and notarial records. The status of Sicilian may be compared to that of the languages of other regions, like Catalonia and Scotland, incorporated into larger nations centuries ago.

Scholars like Giuseppe Pitrè sought to preserve Modern Sicilian by bringing it more firmly into the realm of written languages. More recently, the late Alberto Varvaro, who directed work on a major Sicilian-Italian dictionary, attempted to standardize its orthography. Beyond Italian shores, an effort led by Gaetano Cipolla, a professor of Romance languages, has introduced it to English speakers.

In the field of onomatology, the origins of some Sicilian surnames are mentioned in Joseph Fucilla's *Our Italian Surnames* (1949) and Louis Mendola's *Sicilian Genealogy and Heraldry* (2013).

Middle Sicilian

Here the emphasis is literature rather than oral mastery of a medieval language.

The Poetry of the Sicilian School (1986), by Frede Jensen, is excellent when you can find it. It contains translations of some important poems, with some original texts included.

The Kingdom of Sicily 1100-1250: A Literary History (2005), by Karla Mallette, is a more general survey that includes works in Arabic as well as Sicilian; it presents the English translations but not the texts in their original languages.

Sicily's Rebellion against King Charles (2015), by Louis Mendola, is a translation of the memoir of John of Procida about the War of the Vespers, *Lu Rebellamentu di Sichilia contra Re Carlu* (quoted above). Translated from the *Spinelli Codex* (the oldest known manuscript), this is the earliest known work of narrative prose, rather than verse, written in one of the vernacular "Italian" languages.

In addition to the original text and a Sicilian-English glossary, the book includes the *Contrasto* of Ciullo of Alcamo. This also appears in a newer, more literal translation (accompanied by the original Sicilian text) in Jacqueline Alio's *Queens of Sicily* (2018). By the same authors, *The Peoples of Sicily* has a chapter on the Sicilian language.

The orthography and diacritical marks used in Middle Sicilian, which existed as a literary language before such tongues as Tuscan, are not entirely suitable to Modern Sicilian, and it should be noted that Neapolitan is quite different from Sicilian.

Modern Sicilian

An excellent beginner's course in the language is *Learn Sicilian* (2013) by Gaetano Cipolla. A complementary volume is *Introduction to Sicilian Grammar* (2001) by J. Kirk Bonner and Gaetano Cipolla.

Joseph Bellestri's *Basic Sicilian-English Dictionary* (1985) is a useful study aid, along with his *English-Sicilian Dictionary* (1988). However, since both are out-of-print, it may be necessary to resort to online translation dictionaries. Students already proficient in Italian will benefit from the various Sicilian-Italian dictionaries; one of the better philological references is Alberto Varvaro's two-volume *Vocabolario Storico-Etimologico del Siciliano,* published in 2014.

Some translations of Modern Sicilian works, such as poetry and proverbs, accompanied by the original Sicilian text, are given in the next chapter.

One is unlikely to teach an entire course on Sicilian, just as the study of a subject involving Spain will focus on the national language (Castilian) rather than Catalan. However, a lesson or two introducing Sicilian may be useful if you plan to examine certain Sicilian literature in its original form, and especially if your class will be visiting Sicily.

Some Sicilian words sound a bit like their Italian counterparts but others are quite different.

Imagine the bewilderment of somebody untrained in Sicilian who seeks to interpret a spoken word as commonplace as *piciriddi* (boys, children), or a simple phrase like *lu pisciottu dabànni*, "the young man over there." Some words, like *maniscalco* (blacksmith), for which the Italian is *ferraro,* are now rare. Then there are common words like *parrinu* (priest) and, until recent decades, *fuitina* (a kind of elopement).

Some words are likely to be more understandable in context; *figghiu* is *figlio* (son), *beddu* is *bello* (beautiful), *vastasu* is *sgarbato* (rude), *chistu* is *questo* (this), *nuddu* is *nessuno* (nobody), *joviri* is *giovedì* (Thursday), *cona* is *icona* (icon). However, words like *camurrusu* (annoying), from which *cammuria,* and *cajordu* (vile and dirty) have no direct cognates or translations in Tuscan Italian.

Modern Sicilian has no universal spelling, nor a true future tense.

Interactive resources for learning Modern Sicilian, and for networking with those who advocate for preservation and study of the language, are available on the internet.

Page from the Spinelli Codex *of the* Rebellamentu di Sichilia *written in Middle Sicilian, the oldest surviving Italian prose; this manuscript was the source for Louis Mendola's translation.*

10
ART, MUSIC, LITERATURE, CINEMA

A few works of Sicilian art and literature have been considered in previous chapters. Here the emphasis is placed on what is available in English.

Art

Very little has been published in English about the visual arts in Sicily. Much of what exists is found in contexts such as archeology and architecture. Here the books by Ernst Kitzinger and Otto Demus about the Byzantine mosaics of Sicily come to mind. The Renaissance painting of Antonello da Messina is sometimes mentioned in general anthologies.

Although neither was Sicilian, Caravaggio and Van Dyck both spent time in Sicily, where their work can be seen.

Michael Buonanno's *Sicilian Epic and Marionette Theater* (2014) is a fine study of folk art. A slightly more general work in this area is *The Chivalric Folk Tradition in Sicily: A History of Storytelling, Puppetry, Painted Carts and Other Arts* (2014) by Marcella Croce.

Very little is available in English about Sicilian majolica. In 1877, Arthur Beckwith published his *Majolica and Fayence,* now obtainable in reprint, which considers this art in Sicily.

Music

Even though recordings of the music of classical composers and folk musicians are widely available, little has been written in English about Sicilian music.

An interesting biography of Alessandro Scarlatti (1660-1725) is Edward Dent's book *Alessandro Scarlatti: His Life and Works* (1905).

A fine treatment of Vincenzo Bellini (1801-1835) is *The Life of Bellini* (1996) by John Roselli.

Little exists in English about Antonio Gandolfo Brancaleone (1820-1888).

Ancient and Medieval Literature

A certain *corpus* of classical Greek literature exists that may be described as "Sicilian." This includes the works of Aeschylus, which are available in various editions. The Syracusan dramatist Epicharmus of Kos wrote a play called "The Sausage." Theocritus is credited for creating Greek bucolic poetry. Classicists will need no introduction to this early Siceliot literature.

Ancient mythology was considered in Chapter 5.

As we have seen, there are very few English translations of the medieval literature of Sicily. Presently, these will be found in *The Poetry of the Sicilian School* (1986) by Frede Jensen, *The Kingdom of Sicily 1100-1250: A Literary History* (2005) by Karla Mallette, and *Queens of Sicily 1061-1266* (2018) by Jacqueline Alio. The lengthiest narrative written in Middle Sicilian to be published in English translation is *Sicily's Rebellion against King Charles* (2015), by Louis Mendola.

Shakespeare in Sicily

William Shakespeare's plays *Much Ado About Nothing* and *The Winter's Tale* are set in Sicily. The "Bard of Avon" never visited the island. However, the "Oxfordian Theory" of authorship supported by such scholars as Roger Stritmatter and Charles Beauclerk suggests that the author of the plays may have been Edward de Vere, who did visit Sicily.

Modern Literature

This area offers us far more work in translation. Into the twentieth century, the novels, plays and poems of Sicilian writers stood at the vanguard of Italian literature. The most recognizable names are Giovanni Verga (1840-1922), Luigi Pirandello (1867-1936), Maria Messina (1887-1944), Giuseppe Tomasi di Lampedusa (1896-1957), Salvatore Quasimodo (1901-1968), Vitaliano Brancati (1907-1954), Elio Vittorini (1908-1966) and Leonardo Sciascia (1921-1989). Their work constitutes a *de facto* "canon" of modern Sicilian literature.

This reflects only a partial view because certain works, such as the novels of Luigi Natoli (1857-1941) and Elvira Mancuso (1867-1958), though worthy of consideration, have not yet been published in English.

There are some obvious political implications here. Vittorini and Messina found themselves oppressed by the Fascist regime, their work censored. Pirandello, conversely, was an enthusiastic Fascist.

The Leopard (1960), by Giuseppe Tomasi di Lampedusa, has become something of a modern classic, and its sober view of Italy's unification movement prompted many to question the propaganda that characterized study of the *Risorgimento*. The commercial success of *The Leopard* encouraged the English translation of a very similar novel, which appeared in Italian in 1894; this is *The Viceroys* (1962) by Federico De Roberto. Both focus on the aristocracy.

By contrast, the focus of *The Collected Sicilian Folk and Fairy Tales of Giuseppe Pitrè* (2009), translated by Jack Zipes and Joseph Russo, is folklore.

Another interesting entry is *Sicily, Island of Myths* (2011) by Giuseppe Quatriglio. Very little of this book involves classical mythology, but some popular stories and legends are included.

On an equally whimsical note, an oft-overlooked novella of Giuseppe Tomasi di Lampedusa is *The Professor and the Mermaid*.

Arthur Dieli's *Sicilian Proverbs* (2014) is a good collection with translations and explanations.

Works that have fallen into the public domain can be re-published by anybody. In most cases the years indicated here are merely those of popular, recent editions. Some of these include useful prefatory material.

By Giovanni Verga are *Cavalleria Rusticana and Other Stories* (2000) and *Little Novels of Sicily* (2000), the latter translated by D. H. Lawrence, whose life at Taormina inspired *Lady Chatterley's Lover*. Another fine edition is *Sicilian Stories: A Dual Language book* (2002), translated by Stanley Appelbaum, which features parallel translations that are useful for those studying the Italian language. A fine edition of *The House by the Medlar Tree* was published in 1953 and reissued in 2015.

Luigi Pirandello's plays are available in translation. *Eleven Short Stories by Luigi Pirandello* (1994), translated by Stanley Appelbaum, includes the Italian text. *Six Characters in Search of an Author* (1998) is Pirandello's most famous work. Others are *The Late Mattia Pascal* and *The Oil Jar*.

Vitaliano Brancati wrote a number of works but only a few are currently available in English, namely *Beautiful Antonio* (2007) and *Don Giovanni in Sicily* (2009).

Salvatore Quasimodo has left us much poetry. An excellent recent compilation is *Complete Poems: Salvatore Quasimodo* (2018).

The novels of Leonardo Sciascia, who in later life was active in politics, were known for their gritty realism. Here we have *The Day of the Owl* (2003), *The Wine-Dark Sea* (2000), *To Each His Own* (2000) and *Sicilian Uncles* (2001).

The works of Maria Messina (1887-1944) have been rediscovered and published in translation. These are *Behind Closed Doors: Her Father's House and Other Stories of Sicily* (2007) translated by Elise Magistro, and *A House in the Shadows* (1990) translated by John Shepley.

Outside Italy, Elio Vittorini's most popular work is *Conversations in Sicily,* first published in English in 1949 with an introduction by Ernest Hemingway.

Analyses and critiques of some of these works are available in various publications, both in print and online, and also as introductions in a few editions of these books. Here in Italy, the work of these writers is less popular with a general readership than it once was, even though a few of these novels are required reading in Sicilian schools. Many stories are set in the dark dystopia that existed during the Savoy years, from Garibaldi to Mussolini, an era about which Italians are increasingly indifferent, if not cynical.

Santi Buscemi has translated the work of Luigi Capuana (1839-1915), who wrote in Sicilian. These books are *Sicilian Tales* (2009), *The Marquis of Roccaverdina* (2013) and *Nine Sicilian Plays by Luigi Capuana* (2016).

Giovanni Meli (1740-1816) also wrote in Sicilian. A fine compilation is *The Poetry of Giovanni Meli* (2015) by Gaetano Cipolla.

Not to be overlooked is the work of Domenico Tempio (1750-1821). Here a good translation is Giovanna Summerfield's *Domenico Tempio: Poems and Fables* (2010).

In an earlier time, Antonio Veneziano (1543-1593) wrote in Sicilian. Gaetano Cipolla's *Ninety Love Octaves by Antonio Veneziano* (2006) includes the original text.

There are "literary parks" or other museums dedicated to a few of the more famous Sicilian writers.

An interesting foray into travel literature, and specifically the places described by Sicilian authors and those visiting the island, is *Sicily: A Literary Guide for Travelers* (2014), by Andrew and Suzanne Edwards. A fine exposition that considers numerous writers' perceptions of Sicily over many centuries, it is an excellent survey and a springboard for further reading.

New Literature

A chronological line between "established" (or "traditional") Sicilian literature and "new" literature might be drawn, somewhat arbitrarily, around 1990. It is certainly true that very little modern Sicilian literature was translated into English before then, and that, more generally, Italian literature began to move in new directions toward the end of the twentieth century. It is undeniable that, despite the presence of talented writers, in the eyes of Italian critics, who are notorious curmudgeons, no Sicilian novelist has stepped into the shoes of Giuseppe Tomasi di Lampedusa or Leonardo Sciascia.

Be that as it may, a number of Sicilian authors, such as Andrea Camilleri, merit mention, and the first work of erotic fiction by Melissa Panarello sold well enough, though chiefly in Italy, to become the most widely-read Sicilian novel after *The Leopard*. (Both authors have seen their novels translated into English.) Lara Cardella's *Good Girls Don't Wear Trousers* (1993) is a novel written in the first-person, as if it were a memoir.

New times bring new complexities. Until recently, a contemporary "Sicilian" writer was loosely defined as somebody like Luigi Pirandello whose roots were Sicilian, lived in Sicily (or at least in Italy), and wrote in Italian, perhaps with a few words of Sicilian tossed into the mix. Today we are confronted by two peculiar realities, with many more to come.

Firstly, there is the Sicilian "diaspora" consisting of Sicilian descendants abroad (outside Italy) who do not live in Sicily full-time and do not write in Italian. Here one thinks of the novels of Susan Russo Anderson and Angelo Coniglio featuring stories set in Sicily.

Related to this phenomenon, there are foreign writers who set their stories in Sicily but have not even an ancestral link to the island. Although its author was not Sicilian, *A Bell for Adano* (1944), by John Hersey, draws its inspiration from events in the town of Licata during the Second World War.

Secondly, an increasing number of immigrants, most notably those from Asia and Africa, have made Sicily their home even as many native Sicilians have left the island. We have even met the children of such immigrants who, having been born and raised in Sicily, speak Sicilian! How do we categorize the literary art created by these new sons and daughters of Sicily?

Sicily is not the only place to experience these trends. Clearly, the definitions of "Sicilian literature" and "Sicilian fiction" are evolving.

What is a Sicilian? Is it everybody born in Sicily? Is it anybody descended from people born in Sicily before a certain year? In the twelfth century, people of diverse origins were regarded by the King of Sicily as Sicilians. Until the nineteenth century, Sicily was a sovereign nation whose citizens were identified as *Siciliani*. Today, the gentilic *Siciliano* is not defined in law here in Italy except as an adjective for a few culinary appellations. Unlike, say, Texas, the Sicilian Region does not issue driving licenses or operate universities; the Italian Republic does. There exists residency (based on locality) but not Sicilian citizenship. Even familial identity is defined rather loosely; hereditary rights to titles of nobility and heraldic arms are not recognized or protected (as if they were copyrights or trademarks), and the concept of legitimacy of birth has been abolished in Italy, where some twenty-five percent of the children are born outside marriage. Legally, just as anybody can call himself a baron, anybody can call himself a Sicilian or Calabrian or Tuscan. As we stated at the beginning of this book, there is no unifying Sicilian ethos, ideology, behavior or world view; Sicilians, however we define them, are individuals.

Memoirs

There is not, at present, an assured place for memoirs in the field of Sicilian Studies.

Those seeking to challenge this assertion are likely to proclaim that, by way of example, the diary of Anne Frank and the wartime memoir of Dwight Eisenhower have universal value. Of course they do. So do theme-specific accounts written by, for example, somebody like Danilo Dolci or Filippo Testa, who recount their experiences opposing the Mafia. Memoirs that focus on the experiences of oppressed Sicilian women also have a certain value. Certain it is that the memoirs of Gerre Mangione and Justin Vitiello are informative.

On the other hand, educators and critics (as well as students) may be less inclined to ascribe much significance to the solipsistic story, however interesting, of a foreign woman who comes to Sicily and then recounts her various experiences to anybody who will read about them. We mention this sub-genre because the "innocent female abroad" has become a common theme of memoirs set in Sicily and published in English.

The educator must consider whether a course on Sicilian history or literature need even consider the kind of subjective, anecdotal views embodied in the typical memoir, which may lead readers to infer generalities about Sicily from the specific experience of one person.

Some recent memoirs are worth reading, but are they worth studying?

For the most part, what is found in recent memoirs is not conducive to a productive, educational study of Sicily or Sicilians.

A related genre, the personal travelogue, was more useful in an earlier age, when its author was a traveler like Benjamin of Tudela or bin Jubayr, than today, when the internet makes every visitor an instant, world-famous "expert."

Cinema

Cinema is an area, more so than most of the others mentioned in this book, where language is still a barrier. Some Italian-produced movies set in Italy are actually filmed in English. Nevertheless, only a tiny number of those intended chiefly for domestic (Italian) release are ever dubbed or subtitled for international audiences.

For our purposes, "Sicilian Cinema" shall be loosely, if imperfectly, defined as motion pictures made for general release filmed in Sicily by directors having a close connection to Sicily. The emphasis shall be placed on films available in English, even if the language is presented through subtitles. *The Godfather* films are not, strictly speaking, Sicilian, even though their director is descended from Sicilians; nor would a science fiction movie made by a Sicilian- born director be considered "Sicilian Cinema" unless its story were set in a futuristic Palermo. As an Italian production, *The Leopard* (1963), directed by Luchino Visconti, is arguably more "Sicilian" than *The Sicilian* (1987), directed by Michael Cimino, though both are set in Sicily and include Italian and American actors.

In practice, a profound study of Italian film would necessitate a knowledge of Italian, not only to understand the dialogue, where this is in Italian, but to grasp the nuances inherent in language.

The first Italian film set in Sicily to find a wide international audience was Roberto Rossellini's *Stromboli* (1950), starring Ingrid Bergman.

The themes of Michelangelo Antonioni's *L'Avventura* (1960) are mystery and lust. *Bell'Antonio* was released the same year.

Pietro Germi's *Divorce Italian Style* (1961), starring Marcello Mastroianni, was popular internationally. *The Leopard,* as we have seen, was released in 1963; this starred Burt Lancaster in the title role.

Based on a novel by Leonardo Sciascia, *We Still Kill the Old Way* (1967) is the story of a murder in which the Mafia, the government and even the church are complicit.

Salvatore Samperi's *Malicious* (1973) is a light, lusty comedy set in Sicily.

Several films directed by Giuseppe Tornatore focus on rural Sicily during the twentieth century. *Cinema Paradiso* (1988) won the Academy Award for "Best Foreign Language Film" in 1990. He also directed *The Star Maker* (1995), *Malena* (2000) and *Baarìa* (2009).

Massimo Troisi's film, *Il Postino* (1994), set in Messina and Salina, stars Maria Grazia Cucinotta, one of the few Sicilian actresses known outside Italy.

Roberto Benigni's *Johnny Stecchino* (1991) is a comedy set in Bagheria and Palermo. Benigni went on to win an Oscar for *Life is Beautiful* (1997).

The Sicilian Girl (2009), directed by Marco Amenta, is based on the true story of Rita Atria, a young woman who struggled against the Mafia following the murders of her father and brother.

11
CULINARY CULTURE

Food and wine, and the millennia of history they bear on their shoulders, are an integral part of any culture. Here is where social history, the history of the people, supplants purely political history, with its dry facts and dates.

Mythology and classical history are intertwined with episodes involving agriculture, food and drink. In Sicily, Persephone was associated with the pomegranate and her mother, Demeter (Ceres) with grain. Dionysos (Bacchus), of course, was the god of wine. Apropos wine, a map of Sicilian appellations follows this chapter.

As one would intuit, the recorded culinary history of Sicily is very old. In antiquity, Archestratos, a Greek poet who lived in southeastern Sicily, wrote about the island's cuisine in his *Life of Luxury*. For a fine translation of what fragments of it survive, along with informative commentary, we have *Archestratos of Gela: Greek Culture and Cuisine in the Fourth Century BCE* (2000) by S. Douglas Olson and Alexander Sens. Like many scholarly editions, this one is a bit pricey.

More recently, Francesca Lombardo's *Sicilian Food and Wine: The Cognoscente's Guide* (2015) is the most useful introductory survey of its subjects currently in print. Although it includes a few recipes, this is not a cookbook or "culinary memoir." Rather, it succinctly describes Sicilian culinary history, with more attention to cheeses, olive oil varieties and wines than what is found in most books of this kind. The author is a certified sommelier.

Another book along these lines is *The Art of Sicilian Cooking* (1982) by Anna Muffoletto.

Most of the more popular books about Sicilian food and wine contain too much "personal" information for our taste. They are written much like memoirs. Indeed, an article by Florence Fabricant that appeared in *The New York Times* in May 1991 bears the title "Prose, Not Recipes, Now Sells Food Books," referring to "memoirs with food as their focus." This leads to learning more about the author than you ever wanted to know. Some students may welcome that, but one is cautioned about accepting every anecdote as if it were an ironclad fact.

Are we suggesting that books about food and wine need be devoid of all personal commentary, even the occasional anecdote? Of course not! Francesca Lombardo's guide includes an anecdote at the very beginning of the book, but it is presented as a prologue and separated from the rest of the text. By the same token, a biographical note about the author belongs at the beginning or end of the book, or perhaps on the dust jacket or back cover, not sprinkled throughout the text. We are merely telling you what to expect should you decide to use certain books as part of a course.

Mary Taylor Simeti's *Pomp and Sustenance: Twenty-five Centuries of Sicilian Food* (1989), republished as *Sicilian Food: Recipes from Italy's Abundant Isle,* is essentially a recipe book, but the culinary history presented is solid and fairly detailed. This volume is very useful, and merits credit as one of the few books of Sicilian recipes published in English (as its original language) before 1990. Its only shortcoming is the author's repeated use of the word *peasant* in referring not only to the historical past but to folks she has met, something that may offend some readers.

It took them five or six years, but a few Sicilian women eventually tried to emulate this book. In some cases, their books were connected to promotions for things like cooking lessons. Although the results have been mixed, a few of these more recent publications stand out.

Coming Home to Sicily: Seasonal Harvests and Cooking from Case Vecchie (2012), by Fabrizia Lanza, has the same personal approach. The author's mother, Anna Tasca Lanza, also wrote a cookbook, *The Flavors of Sicily* (1996).

From Wanda and Giovanna Tornabene comes *Sicilian Home Cooking: Family Recipes from Gangivecchio* (2001).

Also worth considering are *Made in Sicily* (2012) by Giorgio Locatelli, *Sicily* (2013) by Pamela Sheldon Johns, and *Sicily: Recipes from an Italian Island* (2016) by Katie and Giancarlo Caldesi.

An interesting memoir that presents some pastry recipes which had not previously been published in English is *Bitter Almonds: Recollections and Recipes from a Sicilian Girlhood* (1994) by Maria Grammatico, who established a famous pastry shop in Erice, and Mary Taylor Simeti.

Elizabeth Gilbert's *Eat, Pray, Love* (2006) has a chapter on Sicilian food which did not make it into the movie starring Julia Roberts.

Some informative volumes focus on wine.

The World of Sicilian Wine (2013), by Bill Nesto and Frances Di Savino, is an excellent oenicultural history and guide. Its authors have a keen sense of Sicily's ancient history.

More succinct and less structured, though interesting, is Robert Camuto's *Palmento: A Sicilian Wine Odyssey* (2012), with its interviews of winemakers. This reads more like a memoir.

Count Filippo Testa, a vintner, brings us a book that pretends to be nothing other than a candid memoir. Coauthored with Susannah Elliott, *The Vine Whisperer* (2017) gives the reader an idea of the challenges confronting a Sicilian wine-maker.

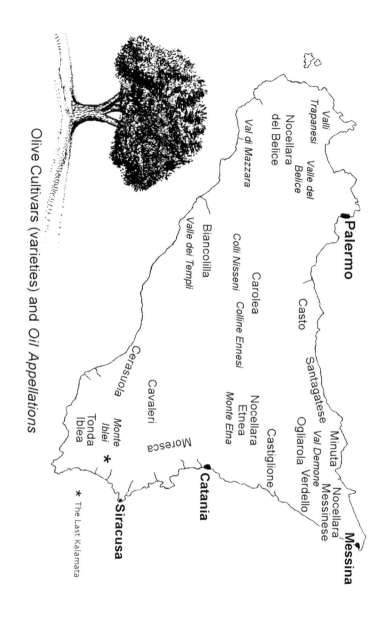

Olive Cultivars (varieties) and *Oil Appellations*

Palermo

Messina

Catania

Siracusa

Valli Trapanesi

Valle del Belice

Nocellara del Belice

Val di Mazzara

Biancolilla

Colli Nisseni

Carolea

Colline Ennesi

Valle dei Templi

Cerasuola

Cavaleri

Moresca

Monte Iblei

Tonda Iblea

Casto

Santagatese

Ogliarola Verdello

Nocellara Etnea

Monte Etna

Castiglione

Minuta

Val Demone

Nocellara Messinese

* The Last Kalamata

179

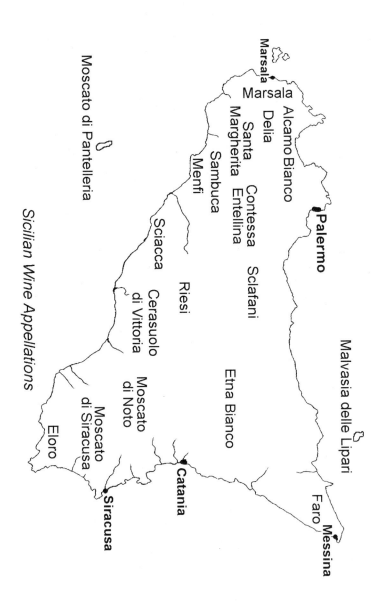

Sicilian Wine Appellations

12
STUDY TOURS

A visit to Sicily can supplement a course or it can provide the setting for credit-bearing lectures. The experience should be planned to be educational, interesting and enjoyable. Before considering details, a few generalities are in order.

Planning

In formulating a visit to Sicily with their students, educators are sometimes inclined to consider "concept" or "thematic" tours that focus on something like ancient archeology, Byzantine art, medieval structures, modern literature or Baroque architecture. For example, a study of modern Sicilian literature might include a visit to a "literary park" or other museum dedicated to a particular Sicilian writer.

That approach may make sense in view of the scope of the course you are teaching, and a specific kind of site can certainly be the emphasis. However, upon realizing how much there is to see in Sicily, even those teaching a course about a particular period usually reconsider the idea, electing to add various sites to the experience.

Rarely is a purely thematic itinerary that is proposed at a tour's planning stage actually put to use. It would be a disservice to students, or any tour group, to see the splendid medieval mosaics at Monreale's cathedral without, if time allows, visiting Segesta to see its imposing Greek temple.

It is usually more convenient to choose lodging in a city rather than on its periphery. It would be ridiculous for the tour participants to have to enlist taxi service just to go out for a pizza in the evening or to explore a city like Palermo during an afternoon at leisure. However, a serene locality like Cefalù or Siracusa, from which excursions can be planned, may be a more suitable base for a three-week course.

For most groups, visiting during the "low " tourism season, from early November into the middle of March, is better than arriving in the hot, crowded "high" season, from early April to the middle of October. Summer is the worst time to visit Sicily for a tour; apart from the huge crowds (and long lines to enter important sites) and torrid heat, many restaurants located in cities away from the beach close for the month of August.

How much time should you spend in Sicily? A week is scarcely enough for a serious tour. For most groups, it's best to dedicate a visit exclusively to Sicily, rather than adding it to a tour of peninsular Italy.

The chief airports are at Palermo and Catania, and an efficient itinerary crosses the island, flying into one city and departing from the other.

In planning a trip, it is worth noting those holidays when some things (even certain historical sites and museums) will be closed: January 1st, January 6th, February 5th (St. Agatha's Day in Catania), Easter Sunday, Easter Monday, April 25th, May 1st, June 2nd, July 15th (St. Rosalie's Day in Palermo), August 15th, November 1st, December 8th, December 25th, December 26th.

Keep in mind that students traveling on passports issued by nations that are not in the visa waiver program (which permits a ninety-day stay) or, alternatively, the European Union will need visas to enter Italy. Many students attending British or American universities are from countries other than these. Applying for a visa should not be left until the last minute because it may take weeks for an Italian consulate to issue one.

Places

Certain choices are fairly obvious. Apart from interesting but "minor" sights (Morgantina's archeological site and Palermo's church of Saint John of the Lepers) of greatest interest to specialist scholars, a number of popular attractions stand out so much that it is almost presumed that you'll visit them when you're in Sicily. These are indicated on the accompanying map.

The focus of Sicilian archeology is decidedly more Greek than Roman. The principal ancient archeological sites, which are the most impressive for their standing temples, are Segesta and Agrigento, followed by Selinunte and the center of Siracusa. There are large Greek theatres at Segesta, Siracusa and Taormina. Sicily has numerous "minor" sites, shown in one of this book's maps ("Eternal Cities").

There are vestiges of Punic and Roman culture as well. The most interesting Roman site in Sicily is the villa at Piazza Armerina, with its extensive mosaic pavements. The most remarkable Punic attraction is certainly the island of Mozia, but Erice was built on an Elymian-Punic site. Even the city of Catania has Roman structures.

The main places to see Norman-Arab architecture, and particularly Byzantine mosaics, are Monreale Abbey, Cefalù Cathedral, the Palatine Chapel in Palermo's Norman Palace, and the Martorana church in the same city. There are numerous other

Norman-Arab landmarks in and around Palermo, and the authors of this book wrote a useful guide to most of these.

Our favorite castles are those of Caccamo, Catania, Mussomeli and Milazzo. The most pleasant historical districts are those of Siracusa, Erice, Cefalù and Taormina.

Here is a list of the more interesting attractions.

Aeolian (Lipari) Islands: These delightful islands are especially appealing in warmer months, but expect large crowds, and limited lodging, in August. In winter ferry service (from Milazzo on the Sicilian coast) is sometimes cancelled for a few days due to bad weather. There are several important archeological sites.

Agrigento: The "Valley of the Temples" is a large archeological site outside town surrounded by olive groves and almond orchards. The almond blossom festival (in late February) is rooted in enchanting folklore. Agrigento boasts several ancient Greek temples, including the Temple of Concord, one of only two completely standing temples in Sicily that survives in anything like its original form. The other is at Segesta, and if time is very limited we suggest visiting either one, rather than both.

Baroque Sicily: The towns of Ragusa and nearby Noto, with their palaces and churches in the Sicilian Baroque style, are something truly representative of eighteenth-century Sicilian architecture and art. The landscapes of the Hyblaean Mountains, and even some of the architecture of these towns, are rather similar to what you encounter in Malta, which really isn't very far away. Beaches and the coastal Vendicari Nature Reserve are an easy driving distance from both cities.

Cefalù: To describe Cefalù as western Sicily's "Taormina" may be a slight overstatement, but it is certainly the most similar thing you'll find. The design of the splendid Norman cathedral was based on a French one, but nothing else in this seaside town owes much to anything other than Sicily's own multicultural influences. There's an ancient Sicanian temple on the rocky cliff overlooking the town, and the ruins of a castle. The town itself offers pleasant, narrow medieval streets and interesting shops. Just an hour from Palermo, Cefalù is a great excursion idea if you're staying in the capital.

Erice: This hilltop town, the ancient Eryx, was successively Elymian, Phoenician, Carthaginian and Roman. Its gray stone forms Punic walls, a castle, churches and medieval streets that could almost be mistaken for ancient ones, bringing to the Good Friday passion procession an atmosphere rarely matched anyplace in Italy or Greece. But there's much more to Erice than this singular annual event. While you're there, don't forget to try the local pastries or couscous.

Mount Etna: Europe's greatest natural wonder is a living, sacred mountain of legend and myth. Consider a jeep excursion to the upper regions, which are covered with snow for four months of the year. Dress warmly in summer too; it's always cool at the top. This is Sicily's highest mountain. Many fine vineyards and wineries will be found on its lower slopes.

Monreale: The arcane fact that a mosaic icon of Thomas Becket graces the apse, and that it is the earliest holy image of the English saint murdered at Canterbury, is just one of many fascinating features of this twelfth-century cathedral and cloister built on a hill in the syncretic Norman-Arab style with Byzantine artistic elements. (Another "secret" detail is that the heart of Saint Louis is preserved here.) No trip to Palermo is really complete without seeing Monreale, which overlooks the city and its vast valley. Plan to spend at least two hours in this peaceful place. You'll rejoice that you did.

Nebrodian Mountains: The Nebrodian Mountains are the most lushly forested region of Sicily. Situated to the immediate north of Etna, the range boasts some of the island's highest peaks after the volcano itself (though several in the Madonian Mountains to the west exceed them). The unique Nebrodian appeal is its complete departure from any common stereotype of "Mediterranean" landscapes and the visitor's consequent realization that much of Sicily looked this way when the first Phoenicians, Ausonians and Greeks arrived millennia ago. Our favourite drive is along the SS 289 from Cesarò high in the mountains to San Fratello and Sant'Agata Militello, a truly lush area that, with its snowfall from late December into February, often looks more Swiss than Sicilian.

Palermo: Sicily's regional capital and largest city is perhaps best compared to a rough, uncut jewel. Its beauty has to be revealed through careful discovery. You'll find this bustling city chaotic and dusty yet interesting. The historic environment of this former royal capital of kings and emirs is largely Baroque with some nuggets of medieval architecture. The Norman Palace, with its stunning Palatine Chapel, is built upon Phoenician walls. There are a number of monasteries and castles, and a magnificent cathedral, as well as art galleries and a fine archeological museum. Monreale is only a few kilometers outside town. Palermo is a great western-Sicilian "base" for excursions (day trips) to Cefalù, Erice, Segesta, Agrigento and the wine country.

Piazza Armerina: The Roman villa outside town has the most extensive mosaic pavements of the ancient Roman world, composed of rural scenes, pictures of flora and fauna, and classical motifs. Most of it is in exceptional condition, looking as if it were completed yesterday. The structure was the home of a wealthy Roman who loved art.

Segesta: We mentioned that Agrigento has one of Sicily's two completely standing Greek temples. The other is at Segesta. Out of justified pride, a few of today's Greeks might disagree, but this is probably the best-preserved ancient Doric temple in what used to be the Greek world. The site's ancient theatre, set on a hill, boasts a magnificent position. If time is very limited, we suggest that you visit either Segesta or Agrigento, rather than both.

Siracusa: Archimedes, Plato and Saint Paul loved Syracuse, and with good reason. It was one of the most important cities of the ancient Greek world, and the most important in Greek and Roman Sicily. It was also one of the most beautiful. The archeological park is extensive, while the old city, Ortygia, with its charming, narrow streets (closed to most traffic), boasts some fascinating treasures. The cathedral was the ancient Temple of Athena, whose columns and walls are still visible throughout the church. Carved into a limestone hypogeum, one of Europe's oldest mikvehs is a special piece of Judaic heritage not to be missed. The city has Sicily's best archeological museum. Among the cognoscenti, Siracusa has developed a reputation as a kind of "intellectual" alternative to tourist-filled Taormina.

Taormina: This mountaintop town overlooking the Ionian coast is Sicily's most famous resort, full of restaurants and shops, with beaches nearby. Its historical side is ubiquitous. The Greek theatre, with its famous panoramic view of Mount Etna and the coast, is used for concerts and plays, and medieval walls enclose the old town's stone streets (many closed to traffic). There are several castles, including Castelmola overlooking Taormina. Ignored by most visitors, Castelmola is well worth a visit. A visit to Etna is a day-long excursion, and if you enjoy nature the Alcantara Gorge is also appealing. Taormina makes a good base for excursions in eastern Sicily.

Wine Country: Sicily's main viticultural region covers a large patch of the western part of the island. Marsala is the commercial center of this scenic region. You can sample Sicilian wines at virtually any restaurant in Sicily, but actually finding the most scenic viticultural landscape can be elusive. Here's a clue. From Salemi, take the SS 188 to Marsala. Along this "secret" route you'll find little traffic but an endless series of gently rolling hills carpeted with vineyards as far as the eye can see. It's a magical place that rivals any grape-growing region in the world in its serene magnificence. It also has what is in some ways a more distinguished history. That's because domesticated grapes were cultivated in Sicily long before they were introduced into France or northern Italy. Segesta and Erice are nearby.

Tour Operators

Working directly with a tour operator based in Sicily is usually more efficient, and even more economical, than going through an "intermediary" agent who, in turn, will work on your tour with a Sicily-based firm anyway.

Many of the Italian firms that advertise themselves on the internet as "tour operators" are not, in fact, registered as such. In other words, they are only partly legal. One of the potential problems with this is that certain types of insurance, such as coverage for non-performance of service (if a firm goes bankrupt a week before your tour begins) are available only to real tour operators, the kind registered as such through the local "chamber of commerce," a public agency.

Lecturers

In most cases, the professor who accompanies a group of students to Italy serves as their chief lecturer. It is sometimes possible to hire a specialist lecturer in Sicily to supplement the lectures or discussions of the students' professor. Truth be told, there are rather few historians in Sicily qualified to lecture foreign students.

In the great majority of cases, a particular travel company works "exclusively" with certain lecturers and guides. Therefore, educators planning a trip should exercise caution in accepting the advice of tour operators or travel agents who may be inclined to make recommendations in that regard. Some tour operators and travel consultants even work with illegal "tour guides" (described in the next section). The reasoning behind these trends need not concern us; it may suffice to say that economic motives are usually involved, as a good lecturer will require a dignified speaker's fee (honorarium), while a licensed guide will expect the daily rate that is the standard for the profession. In seeking to offer you a competitive price, some tour companies economize on the services of lecturers and guides.

Depending on the subject, finding a competent lecturer on the internet is not impossible. However, some fields lend themselves to improvisation by *soi-disant* "experts." Lecturing visitors about such topics as food, wine or the Mafia has become a cottage industry in Sicily, with mixed results.

As we noted in the first chapters, it is only rarely practical to enlist Sicily-based professors as lecturers because, apart from questions of expertise, few speak English well enough to converse effectively with anglophone students, or even with Chinese, Russian or German students who speak English proficiently as a second language. This means hiring an interpreter, which entails additional expense.

Language aside, some Italian academics have obvious problems socializing with foreigners, perhaps feeling free (under the guise of unsolicited "political opinions") to utter openly derogatory remarks about the United Kingdom or the United States, something that greatly detracts from your group's experience.

Apart from this, there are at least a few English-speaking tour guides in Sicily who are more knowledgeable about certain historical topics than many Sicilian university professors. An example that comes to mind is an Israeli based in Messina who specializes in tours that focus on Sicily's Judaic heritage.

Under Italian law, a professor can lecture students from his own university (if it is in the European Union) at certain historical sites. The legal intricacies of this are too complex to recite at length here, but it is almost always necessary to be accompanied by a tour guide when visiting such places.

Tour Guides

In Italy, this is a licensed profession. Obtaining a tour guide license requires earning a university degree in a relevant area of study, achieving proficiency in a foreign language, and then passing a rigorous exam.

In hiring a tour guide, competence is key. Only *licensed* tour guides are ever recommended. This is a *guida abilitata*. By law, these are the *only* guides authorized to lecture visitors at cathedrals, museums and archeological sites.

Given the magnitude of Italy's "underground" economy, it is hardly surprising that there are also *illegal* tour guides. Illegal "guides" are not even authorized to lecture in the streets and squares immediately outside historical edifices, and certainly not inside, nor can they lecture at archeological sites. Certain trip-planning websites fail to distinguish between legitimate (licensed) guides and illegal ones.

Because the amateur, self-styled "guides" are not authorized by law to lecture at such sites as the cloister of Monreale Abbey or the Agrigento archeological area (where they risk being fined by police), their services are all but useless. Most of their clientele consists of couples or very small groups.

The better your lecturers and guides, the better your group's experience will be.

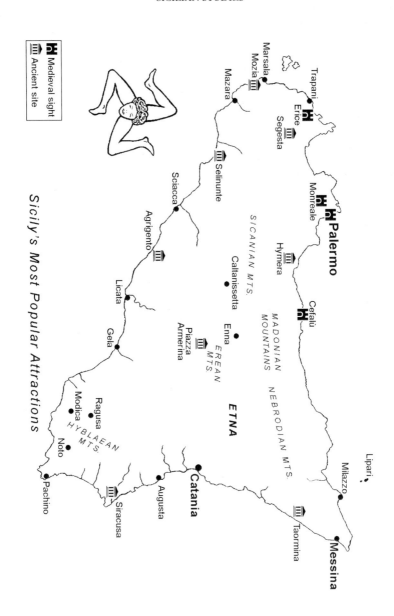

APPENDIX 1

Timeline

Prehistory

9000 BC (BCE) - Superstructures of first megalithic temples at Göbekli Tepe, near Urfa, formerly Edessa, in Anatolia (Turkey), were erected around this time. Incised cave drawings at Addaura (outside Palermo) and Levanzo have been dated approximately to this period. The cave paintings on Levanzo are the oldest such art in Italy.

8000 BC (BCE) - Probable introduction of agriculture (initially wheat and other grains) in Sicily by eastern Mediterranean neolithic farmers, likely predecessors of earliest Indo- Europeans identified genetically with M172 (J2) haplogroup that originated in Fertile Crescent. Neolithic jewelry crafted in Sicily.

4000 BC (BCE) - Proto Sicanians inhabit Sicily and Malta. On Malta and Gozo they build Europe's oldest free-standing structures at Zebbug, Gantija, Mnajdra, Hagar Qim and Tarxien, and invent the simple wheel (a stone cylinder fitted to a semicylindrical groove carved into a stone block), leaving behind a large hypogeum and various artworks. Earliest Sicilian religion practiced. Equally advanced Minoan (Cretan and Aegean) civilization flourishes in eastern Mediterranean.

Native History: Sicanians, Elymians, Sikels

2000 BC (BCE) - Sicanian culture dominant in Sicily. Use of copper tools ("Early Bronze Age"), possibly indicating non-Sicilian influences, was prevalent by 2500 BC. Mycenaean and Late Minoan cultures present in isolated eastern localities.

1800 BC - Birth of Abraham according to Hebrew tradition (approximate dating).

1500 BC - Extensive Mycenaean trade with Sikels of Aeolian (Lipari) Islands and parts of the Ionian coast (at Thapsos) and Sicanians. Ausonians, an Italic people, also trade with Aeolian islanders.

1400 BC - Iron Age begins in Greece. Estimated arrival date of Sikels (Sicels), an Italic people, in eastern Sicily.

1330 BC - Birth of Moses according to Hebrew tradition.

1303 BC - Birth of Ramesses II, Pharaoh of Egypt; references in Book of Exodus may be to another personage.

1200 BC - Elymians (probably from Anatolia in Asia Minor), arrive in western Sicily, founding Segesta (their Egesta), Erice (Eryx), Entella (outside Contessa Entellina), Hypana (usually identified with a site near Prizzi), probably Iaitas (near San Giuseppe Jato). Probable period of introduction of domesticated olive cultivars in Sicily by peoples of Aegean cultures.

1000 BC - Indo-European languages and societies identified to this era based on linguistic similarities.

Phoenicians, Carthaginians and Greeks

840 BC (BCE) - Foundation of Carthage according to most estimates.

775 BC - Greek trading settlement on Ischia becomes their first in southern Italy. Phoenician port of Motya (Mozia near Marsala) may have been founded around this time.

750 BC - Phoenicians establish Zis (Palermo) and Kfra (Solunto) as trading centers.

735 BC - Naxos founded as first permanent Greek colony in Sicily.

733 BC - Syracuse (Siracusa) founded as Greek colony.

705 BC - Greeks assimilate Sikels' city of Enna, with which myth of Persephone becomes identified.

612 BC - Phoenicia falls to Chaldean (Neo-Babylonian) Empire, leaving Carthage as Phoenicians' major city.

580 BC - Akragas (Agrigento) founded.

504-466 BC - Hippocrates and Gelon (from 478), as Tyrants of Syracuse, rule most of eastern Sicily.

490 BC - Athenians defeat Persians at Battle of Marathon. Persian Wars begin, lasting until 479.

480 BC - Carthaginians (encouraged to fight the Greeks by Xerxes of Persia who has won victories in Greece) are defeated by Gelon of Syracuse at first Battle of Hymera. Persians defeated at Battle of Salamis.

474 BC - Syracusans win naval victory over Etruscans at Cumae.

415-413 BC - Athenians invade eastern Sicily during Peloponnesian War, defeated by Syracusans in 413.

410-405 BC - Carthaginians invade western Sicily, destroying Hymera in 409, establishing permanent military presence at Zis (Palermo). Wars between Carthaginians and Greeks (and subsequently with Romans) continue.

409 BC - Birth of Dion, later *Tyrant* (leader) of Syracuse.

405-367 BC - Dionysius I rules as Tyrant of Syracuse

398 BC - Plato suggests Sicily as model of utopian society. Syracuse has emerged as Sicily's most important city and will remain so until the 10th century when Arabs and Berbers repopulate Panormos as *Bal'harm* (Palermo).

Roman Period

264 BC (BCE) - First Punic War (Romans against Carthaginians), ending in 241. Second Punic War in 218, ending in 201.

261 BC (BCE) - Romans take Akragas (Agrigento) from Carthaginians.

227 BC (BCE) - Sicily becomes first Roman province but Syracuse resists annexation.

218 BC (BCE) - Carthaginian leader Hannibal invades Italy during Second Punic War.

212 BC (BCE) - Syracuse finally falls to Romans; Archimedes is killed.

146 BC (BCE) - Romans defeat Carthaginians in Third Punic War, which began three years earlier. Romans rename *Panormos* Latin *Panormus*. Earliest continuous Jewish communities in eastern Sicily.

136-132 BC (BCE) - Slave revolt led by Eunus with base at Enna. Slaves conquer large area before defeat by Roman legions.

104-100 BC (BCE) - Slave revolt led by Salvius (Triphon).

70 BC (BCE) - Cicero prosecutes Verres, corrupt Governor of Sicily.

31 BC (BCE) - Octavian (Augustus) rules Rome alone following Battle of Actium.

23 BC (BCE) (circa) - Diodorus Siculus, Siceliot historian, dies.

6 BC (BCE) (circa) - Birth of Jesus.

AD (CE) 14 - Death of Augustus. Established *Pax Romana* lasting until AD (CE) 180. In Augustus' time Romans establish maritime trade with southern India.

AD (CE) 33 (circa) - Death of Jesus.

AD (CE) 59 (circa) - Paul of Tarsus preaches in Syracuse *en route* to Rome, possibly at site of Saint Marcian's Crypt.

AD (CE) 251 - Saint Agatha martyred; later venerated as patroness of Catania.

AD (CE) 303-306 - Diocletian's persecution of Christians. Saint Lucy (of Syracuse) martyred.

AD (CE) 306 - Constantine the Great rules until 337.

AD (CE) 313 - Constantine's "Edict of Milan" permits open practice of Christianity.

AD (CE) 324 - Imperial city of Constantinople (Byzantium) founded on site of older settlement.

AD (CE) 325 - Council of Nicaea defines Christian canon and doctrine, condemns Arianism as heresy. By now Syracuse is Christianized.

AD (CE) 330 - Capital of Roman Empire transferred to Byzantium (Constantinople). *Codex Sinaiticus* written; it is the most complete, earliest surviving copy of the Gospels, as opposed to fragments. *Codex Vaticanus* dates from the same period.

AD (CE) 380 - Christianity official religion of Roman Empire.

AD (CE) 395 - Following death of Theodosius I, Roman Empire definitively splits into Western ("Latin") and Eastern ("Byzantine") administrations. Sicily begins in West but will vacillate between the two.

Vandalic-Gothic Period

406 - Vandals, Sueves, Burgundians and other tribes cross the Rhine. "Great Invasion" has begun.

410 - Visigothic sack of Rome (no longer the capital) under Alaric; political fall of Western Roman Empire begins.

429 - Vandals under Genseric (Gaiseric) invade Roman province of Africa, within striking distance of Sicily.

440 - Vandal invasion leads to mass raids in western Sicily. Their advance is halted by Byzantines in 441.

455 - Vandals sack Rome.

461 - Vandals return to Sicily in long series of raids.

468 - Complete Vandalic occupation of Sicily, lasts until 491. Vandals destroy synagogue at Syracuse.

476 - Odoacer, probably German, deposes Romulus Augustulus, last (western) Roman Emperor. Beginning of Middle Ages usually dated from this time. Genseric, ruler of Sicily and Tunisia, concludes "perpetual" peace with Constantinople.

491 - Ostrogoths achieve complete control of Sicily, ousting Vandals. Their leader, Theodoric, kills Odoacer in 493.

Byzantine Period

527-565 - Rule of Justinian I as Eastern Roman ("Byzantine") Emperor. With *Corpus Juris Civilis* (popularly the "Code of Justinian"), *Epitome Juliani* and other issuances, establishes lasting legal code through gradual implementation in localized forms.

533-535 - Byzantines under Belisarius defeat Vandals (in Tunisia) and Ostrogoths (in Sicily) and annex Sicily to Byzantine Empire. Gothic rule of Sicily ends except for brief incursion and occupation of some localities in 550.

537 - Saint Sophia Basilica built in Constantinople; world's largest church epitomizes Byzantine culture.

570 - Birth of Mohammed, founder of Islam as Prophet.

622 - Hijri calendar based on dating from this year marking Hijrah of Mohammed.

632 - Death of Mohammed.

652 - Small Muslim-Arab force lands in Sicily but soon departs.

655 - Jews of Syracuse begin construction of their large mikveh around this date.

660-668 - Constans II rules Byzantine Empire from Syracuse. Launches failed attempt to reconquer peninsular Italy from the Longobards (Lombards).

661 - Umayyad caliphate established in Damascus.

670 - Arabs conquer most of Tunisia and Libya, establishing Islamic province of Ifriqiya.

698 - Arabs conquer Carthage and environs.

711 - Arabs invade Spain. Island of Pantelleria annexed to Ifriqiya around this time. Arab raids on Sicilian coasts until 734.

726-787 - Iconoclast Controversy.

740 - Arabs briefly occupy Syracuse but must return to Tunisia to quell Berber revolt. Byzantines defeat Arabs at Akroinon in Anatolia.

750 - Abbasids seize Tunisia and Libya from Umayyads of Damascus.

752 - Arabs attack Syracuse.

762 - Abbasid caliphate establishes Baghdad as capital.

768 - Local Muhallabids rule Ifriqiya under Abbasids until 793.

771 - Charlemagne becomes King of the Franks.

774 - Charlemagne occupies Lombard lands in northern Italy.

Aghlabid Period

797 - Following rebellions against the Muhallabids, general Ibrahim ibn al-Aghlab restores order in Ifriqiya.

800 - Abbasid Caliph Harun al-Rashid grants Ifriqiya to Ibrahim ibn al-Aghlab as a hereditary emir, establishing Aghlabid dynasty. Aghlabids are Sunnis who introduce principles of Maliki law.

826 - Euphemius, general in Sicily disgruntled with Byzantine Emperor Michael II, offers control of Sicily to Aghlabids in return for political asylum.

827 - First major Arab-Berber incursion (over 10,000 men sailing from Tunisia, including some Persians) arrives in July under Asad ibn al-Furat, general of Aghlabid Emir Ziyadat Allah I ibn Ibrahim of Ifriqiya. Mazara is occupied.

831 - In September Bal'harm (Palermo) is conquered by Aghlabids following a year-long siege. Island administered by governors.

831-838 - Continued rule of much of Sicily by Ziyadat Allah I, who sponsored al-Furat's invasion in 827.

863 - Rule of Ziyadat Allah II ibn Abil-Abbas. During 9th century Arabs introduce mulberries (for silk making), oranges, rice, sugar cane and other crops, and superior irrigation systems.

878 - Jafar ibn-Mohammed conquers Syracuse, Byzantine capital of Sicily.

881 - *Codex Vigilanus* compiled in Spain, uses Hindu-Arabic numerals.

Fatimid Period

910 - Fatimids now rule Sicily and major Berber revolts begin against this dynasty. Cluniacs founded, follow Benedictine Rule.

913 - Emir Ahmed ibn-Kohrob declares independence of Sicily, evicting Fatimid governor from Bal'harm, but troops of Fatimid ruler, Abdul'Allah al-Mahdi Billah (Said ibn Husayn), restore the island to their dominion.

915 - Arab troops defeated at mouth of Garigliano River south of Rome by forces of Pope, Lombards and Byzantines.

937 - Construction of large mosque, citadel and palaces begins in Palermo's coastal Khalesa district (now the Kalsa).

938 - Last in a series of violent, anti-Fatimid revolts by the Berbers of southwestern Sicily suppressed at Agrigento.

941 - Rus-Byzantine War.

Kalbid Emirate (under Fatimids)

948 - Fatimids (who decide to move their capital) entrust Sicily to local Kalbids, who, like the Fatimids, are Shiites. Emirate of Sicily founded despite rivalry among Sicily's local emirs.

948-954 - Rule of Emir Hassan al-Kalbi, appointed by Fatimid Caliph Ismail al-Mansur. First *kanats* built under Palermo.

964 - Byzantine incursion to support Greeks rebelling at Rometta.

967 - Sicilian-born Jawhar al-Siqilli founds Al-Qahira (Cairo) in name of Fatimids.

972 - Mohammed ibn Hawqal visits Sicily. Observes paper making.

998-1019 - Rule of Ja'far al-Kalbi. Construction of Favara palace in Palermo is attributed to this Emir.

1000 - Norse civilization in northwestern France (Normandy) assimilates with local culture. Approximate period of Norse landings at L'Anse aux Meadows in Newfoundland. *Groenlendinga Saga* (the Greenlanders' Saga) and *Eiriks Saga* (Erik's Story) mention such sea travels.

1016 - Norman knights first participate in battles in Italy. First Turkish raids in Armenia.

1019-1037 - Rule of Ahmed al-Akhal in Sicily.

1037-1040 - Rule by Abdallah Abu Hafs, usurper.

1038-1042 - Byzantine forces of George Maniakes briefly occupy parts of eastern Sicily; army includes Greeks, Normans, Lombards and Norse Varangian Guard under Harald Hardrada.

1040 - Hasan as-Samsam begins his rule; deposed in 1044.

1044 - Island divided into four qadits. Rivalry among emirs worsens.

1053 - Following death of Hasan as-Samsam and extinction of Kalbid dynasty, three important emirs divide control of Sicily: Ibn al Hawas at Kasr' Janni (Enna), Ibn at Timnah at Syracuse and Catania, Abdullah ibn Hawqal at Trapani and Mazara.

1054 - Great Schism between eastern and western Christianity. Sicilian Christians initially remain "eastern" (Orthodox).

1056 - Arab poet ibn Hamdis born; leaves Sicily in 1078.

Norman Period

1060 - Unsuccessful Norman attack in coastal northeastern Sicily.

1061 - Battle of Messina. City and parts of Nebrodian and Peloritan region occupied; permanent Norman presence.

1066 - Battle of Hastings leads to complete Norman conquest of Saxon England. Battle of Messina forms partial pattern of this invasion of an island from a continent; some Norman knights fight at both battles.

1071 - Byzantines lose Battle of Manzikert to Seljuk Turks. Normans attack Palermo; Norman invaders are led by Robert de Hauteville, Arab defenders by Ayub ibn Temim.

1072 - Battle of Palermo ends in early January with Norman occupation under Roger and Robert de Hauteville. Greek Orthodox Bishop Nicodemus removed from authority over Christian community.

1081 - Suppression of revolt led by renegade "emir" Bernavert (Bin al Wardi) at Catania; another of his revolts is suppressed at Syracuse in 1085.

1083 - Roger I appoints Latin (rather than Orthodox) Bishop of Palermo and Gallican Rite is introduced in new churches.

1084 - Bruno founds Carthusian Order in Germany.

1087 - Ibn Hammud, Emir of Kasr' Janni (Enna), last major Arab stronghold, surrenders to Normans in 1087; Noto falls in 1091. Dozens of fortified Arab-founded (or repopulated) towns dot the island: Calascibetta, Caltanissetta, Caltagirone, Mussomeli, Marsala (Mars' Allah), Misilmeri, Cammarata, others.

1095 - Roger II, future King of Sicily, is born.

1096 - First Crusade begins; some Norman knights participate under Bohemond de Hauteville (later Prince of Antioch), brother of Roger I.

1097 - Odo of Bayeux, Earl of Kent, younger brother of William the Conqueror, King of England, dies in Palermo *en route* to the Crusade while visiting Roger I.

1098 - Roger I, as Great Count of Sicily, becomes Papal Apostolic Legate, with rights to approve island's Catholic bishops.

1099 - Crusaders conquer Jerusalem.

1101 - Roger I dies, succeeded by Simon, his eldest living, legitimate son, who is still a minor. Roger's consort, Adelaide del Vasto of Savona, is regent.

1105 - Roger II succeeds his elder brother Simon (1093-1105) as ruler of Sicily under Adelaide's regency.

1112 - Roger II reaches age of majority and sovereign authority following "regency" under his mother.

1119 - Knights Templar founded in Palestine. Preceptories in Sicily confiscated by Frederick II following Sixth Crusade. (Order suppressed definitively by Papacy in 1312.)

1123 - First Lateran Council forbids Roman Catholic clerics wives or concubines; until now Catholic priests were permitted to marry before ordination.

1130 - Roger crowned first King of Sicily (known henceforth as "Roger II").

1139 - Second Lateran Council makes celibacy mandatory for Roman Catholic priests, reiterating a canon established in 1123 but not widely enforced.

1140 - Assizes of Ariano, important legal code asserting royal authority, traditionally dated to this year.

1143 - Martorana church (Palermo) built in Norman-Arab style for Greek Orthodox community by George of Antioch. In this year Nilos Doxopatrios authors theological treatise.

1147 - Second Crusade begins but participation by Sicilian knights is very limited.

1154 - *Book of Roger* completed by court geographer Abdullah al Idrisi. Roger dies and reign of King William I "the Bad" begins.

1155 - Frederick Barbarossa crowned Holy Roman Emperor.

1158 - Qaid al Brun (Thomas Brown), treasurer at William's court, returns to England to reform exchequer of Henry II, thus influencing European accounting principles. He uses Hindu-Arabic numerals, later popularized in Christian Europe by Leonardo Fibonacci of Pisa (briefly a guest of young Frederick II in Sicily) in 1202.

1161 - Matthew Bonellus of Caccamo leads revolt of Norman barons. He is killed in the same year.

1166 - Reign of young King William II "the Good" begins under his mother's regency. Queen Margaret gives hospitality to exiled kin of Thomas Becket. Gradual Latinization of Sicilian language continues; Roman Catholic influence predominates in Christianity.

1169 - Major earthquake in Catania and southeast.

1170 - Benjamin of Tudela visits Sicily. Peter Waldo establishes evangelical Waldensian church, precursor of Reform (Protestant) movement.

1171 - Saladin defeats Fatimids in Middle East.

1174 - Work begins on Monreale Abbey in Arab village of Bal'at overlooking Palermo. Style is Norman-Arab on Romanesque plan with Byzantine mosaic icons, including earliest holy image of Thomas Becket (canonized in 1173).

1177 - William II marries Joanna, daughter of Henry II of England (sister of Richard Lionheart).

1184 - Bin Jubayr visits Sicily and records his impressions.

1187 - Saladin captures Jerusalem.

1189 - Death of William II. Succeeded by Tancred Hauteville.

1190 - Richard Lionheart, brother of Queen Joanna of Sicily, occupies Messina with Philip II of France for several months *en route* to Third Crusade.

1193 - Death of Saladin.

Swabian Period

1194 - Death of Tancred. Holy Roman Emperor Henry VI von Hohenstaufen arrives. Teutonic Order of knights, accompanies him, establishing Saint Mary of the Germans (Messina) and obtaining Cistercian properties (the Magione in Palermo).

1198 - Frederick II, son of Henry, is king until 1250. Swabian German influences in Sicily. Islam and Greek Orthodoxy permitted but practiced by ever-diminishing minorities. Emergent Sicilian language is Latin-based with Arabic and Greek influences.

1204 - Latins ("Franks") sack Constantinople during Fourth Crusade, establish "Latin Empire."

1206 - Mongols unite under Genghis Khan (Temujin), who conquers large parts of Eurasia.

1210 - Francis of Assisi meets Pope Innocent III; founds Order of Friars Minor (Franciscans). Albigensian Crusades begin.

1212 - Frederick II reaches age of majority.

1215 - *Magna Carta* in England. Dominic of Osma (of Caleruega, Spain) founds Order of Preachers (Dominicans or "Blackfriars"), confirmed by Papacy in 1216. By 1500 this is the leading monastic and teaching order in Sicily, supportive of the Inquisition.

1217 - Cleric and scientist Michael Scot (born 1175) translates *On the Sphere* by the Arab astronomer Al-Bitruji (or Alpetragius, who died circa 1204). Fifth Crusade begins.

1220 - Frederick issues Assizes of Capua.

1223 - Following execution of Arab rebel leader Morabit (in 1222), thousands of Arabs from Iato area, who had revolted with their leader Ibn Abbad (or Benaveth), are deported to Lucera in Apulia. Many Muslims have already converted to Catholicism. Jews from occupied Jerba (in Tunisia) invited to Sicily.

1224 - University of Naples founded by Frederick II.

1226 - Frederick II summons Imperial Diet of Cremona.

1229 - Frederick II, accompanied by Saracen guards and Sicilian and German knights, goes on Sixth Crusade as King of Jerusalem. Signs peace with Muslims without war.

1230 - Upon his return from Jerusalem Frederick suppresses Templar preceptories in Sicily.

1231 - Constitutions of Melfi become legal code for Kingdom of Sicily under Frederick II.

1233 - Cathars of France persecuted as heretics by first Inquisition.

1240 - Ciullo of Alcamo composes poetry in Sicilian language. First of a series of revolts by Sicilian Arabs, including some Christian converts, but Frederick retains trusted Saracen guards and court officers.

1241 - Mongol-Tatar army of Batu Khan arrives in central Europe after having sacked Kiev. Leads to foundation of "Golden Horde."

1244 - Fall of Jerusalem to Muslim forces.

1248 - Crusade to Egypt by Louis IX of France.

1250 - Death of Frederick II.

1254 - Death of Conrad IV Hohenstaufen.

1258 - Baghdad falls to Mongols.

Angevin Period

1266 - Charles of Anjou (brother of Louis IX of France) becomes king of Naples and Sicily following defeat of Manfred Hohenstaufen, natural son of Frederick II, at Battle of Benevento.

1268 - Young Conradin, a (legitimate) grandson of Frederick II and last Swabian claimant, is executed in 1268 following defeat at Battle of Tagliacozzo. Hohenstaufen Imperial line now extinct. Angevin period begins. It is thought that by now all of Sicily's remaining Muslims have converted to Catholicism. The multicultural golden age is ending.

1270 - Following Eighth (or "Tunisian") Crusade, funeral of Louis IX of France at Monreale, where his heart is preserved; canonized in 1297.

1273 - Rudolf of Hapsburg becomes king in Germany; his dynasty will succeed Hohenstaufens as Holy Roman Emperors.

Aragonese Period

1282 - Vespers revolt expels Angevin French and makes Peter III of Aragon King of Sicily. Neapolitan invasion of Constantinople is aborted as military resources must be diverted to Sicily. Though sometimes ruled by the same monarch (as a "personal union"), kingdom founded in 1130 remains divided into the peninsular ("Naples") and insular ("Sicily") realms until 1816.

1285 - Deaths of Charles I of Anjou and Peter III of Aragon, succeeded by their sons.

1302 - Peace of Caltabellotta treaty signed between Aragonese and Angevins. By now, Sicily is essentially monocultural and mostly Roman Catholic. Over the next few generations general literacy diminishes.

1306 - Beginning of a "Little Ice Age" in Europe.

1307 - Templars suppressed by King Philip IV "the Fair" of France but the estates of this order had already been confiscated in Sicily by Frederick II, ending its presence on the island.

1309-1377 - Avignon Papacy; Papal court in France. Western Schism follows from 1378 until 1417.

1315-1317 - Bad harvests due to wet, cool Spring and Summer lead to food shortages and Great Famine.

1321 - Dante Alighieri's *Inferno* (part of his *Divine Comedy*) mentions several Popes, Frederick II and Frederick's chancellor Pietro della Vigna (1190-1249).

1337 - Hundred Years' War begins between England and France; English invade France in 1346. (This was actually a series of conflicts rather than a single war.)

1347 - Genoan ships arriving at Messina from eastern Mediterranean bring bubonic plague ("Black Death") to Europe, killing some 20 million Europeans.

1353 - Giovanni Boccaccio's *Decameron* mentions Palermo's Cuba palace and King William II of Sicily.

1361 - A second wave of bubonic plague in Europe.

1377 - Chaos following death of King Frederick "the Simple" until arrival of his dynastic successor King Martin continues until 1392. Chiaramonte, Alagona, Peralta and Ventimiglia families (the "Four Vicars") usurp royal authority, sparking a feudal "civil war." Andrew Chiaramonte is eventually beheaded.

1380 - Tatars defeated at Kulikovo by Russians commanded by Dimitri Donskoy (who completed construction of the Kremlin in 1367).

1397 - Sweden, Denmark and Norway united by Treaty of Kalmar until 1523.

Castilian Period

1412 - House of Aragon succeeded by Trastámara dynasty of Castile based on Compromise of Ceuta.

1415 - Battle of Agincourt results in English victory.

1416 - Alfonso V "the Magnanimous" crowned King of Aragon, Sicily, later (1442) Naples, establishing diplomatic relations with burgeoning Ethiopian Empire and becoming important patron of the Renaissance.

1434 - University of Catania founded.

1447 - Johannes Gutenberg invents printing press using movable type; prints Bible in 1455. (Rudimentary printing plates were developed earlier in China but this publication marks beginning of mass publication.)

1453 - End of Hundred Years' War. Constantinople falls to Ottomans. Conclusion of Middle Ages usually dated to this year, but sometimes to 1492 or 1500. Renaissance has begun. Sicilian-born painter Antonello da Messina is part of this new movement.

1466 - Francesco Laurana, Renaissance sculptor, establishes workshop in Palermo.

1474 - Massacre of over 300 Jews at Modica who refused to pray in a Catholic church.

Spanish Period

1478 - Spanish Inquisition begins; in Sicily it lasts until 1782.

1492 - Edict against Jews (the "Alhambra Decree") forces widespread conversions and some emigrations in 1493. Albanian refugees arrive following Turkish invasions of Balkans. Spanish rule continues in Sicily until 1700s. Columbus lands in America, initiating European colonization.

1497 - Tribunal of the Inquisition ("Holy Office") formally instituted in Palermo to try "heretics."

1516 - Holy Roman Emperor Charles V, King of Spain and ruler of much of western Europe, becomes King of Sicily.

1526 - Outbreak of plague.

1530 - To protect Sicily from pirates and Turks, Charles V cedes Malta to Knights of Saint John ("Knights of Malta") as fief for annual feudal rent of a Maltese falcon.

1548 - Jesuits found their first *studium,* the future University of Messina.

1571 - European Christian fleet gathered at Messina defeats Turks at Lepanto.

1575 - Plague outbreak in Palermo.

1592 - Famine in western Sicily.

1606 - Wheat shortage.

1618 - Thirty Years' War begins. Sicily is involved as part of Spanish Empire.

1624 - Plague ends at Palermo after bones of Saint Rosalie are discovered, but her historicity is questioned by later historians.

1638 - Head tax imposed in Sicily to defray Spanish military expenses of Thirty Years' War.

1647 - Food riots in Palermo due to poor harvest and inefficient agricultural policy of landholders and government. A similar riot follows in Naples.

1651 - *Donativo* tax levied.

1669 - Major eruption of Mount Etna destroys several towns and reaches the Ionian coast at Catania.

1674 - Localized revolt in Messina by the city's oligarchs.

1681 - *Donativo* levied.

1693 - An exceptionally destructive earthquake strikes eastern Sicily, particularly Catania, Noto, Ragusa. Districts are rebuilt in new Sicilian Baroque architecture.

Savoyard and Austrian Rule

1713 - With Treaty of Utrecht Sicily comes under Savoy rule.

1714 - *Donativo* levied by King Vittorio Amedeo.

1718 - British fleet defeats Spanish at Battle of Cape Passaro. Spanish fleet defeats Austrians at Battle of Milazzo during War of the Quadruple Alliance.

1719 - Spanish troops defeat Austrians at Battle of Francavilla. Some 5,000 were killed or wounded in one of the largest land battles fought in Sicily since antiquity. Austrians then besiege Messina, which surrenders.

1720 - Sicily falls under Hapsburg rule as a condition of the Treaty of the Hague. (Savoys lose Sicily but become Kings of Sardinia.)

The Two Sicilies

1734 - Charles of Spain becomes King of Naples and Sicily (and Duke of Parma) following invasion, crowned in Palermo in 1735.

1743 - An epidemic strikes Messina.

1748 - *Donativo* levied by King Charles.

1754 - Italy's first university chair/department in economics established at Naples.

1759 - King Charles of Bourbon becomes Carlos III of Spain. Separates Spanish Crown from those of Naples and Sicily, ceding Italian dominions to his emancipated son, Ferdinand I.

1764 - Famine strikes Sicily following bad wheat harvest.

1767 - Jesuits expelled from kingdoms of Naples and Sicily.

1776 - United States declares independence from Great Britain; France and Spain support Americans.

1778 - San Leucio (near Caserta) becomes first public housing complex/estate in Italy.

1779 - Precursor of University of Palermo founded as *Regia Accademia degli Studi San Ferdinando.*

1782 - Spanish Inquisition abolished in Sicily.

1783 - Peace of Paris treaties signed by Britain, France, Spain and United States end American Revolutionary War.

1788 - First public school for the deaf in Italy established in Naples (school founded in Rome in 1784 was private).

1789 - French Revolution begins.

1795 - First public botanical gardens in Italy open in Palermo (others were private or scholastic). Revolt in Palermo suppressed.

1796 - King of Naples and Sicily recognizes the United States of America; full diplomatic relations established in 1832.

1798 - Malta, part of the Kingdom of Sicily, occupied by Napoleonic fleet which expels Knights of Saint John. Following Britain's victory over the French, Malta and Gozo become British protectorate in 1800 and are never returned to Sicilian Crown.

1799 - Parthenopean Republic declared in Naples. Ferdinand I resides in Palermo.

1801 - Dwarf planet Ceres discovered based on work at astronomical observatory atop Palermo's Norman Palace.

1802 - Ferdinand I returns to Naples during Peace of Amiens.

1803 - Napoleonic Wars begin, end in 1815.

1804 - Jesuits restored in Kingdom of Naples.

1806 - British troops are based in Sicily as bulwark against possible Napoleonic invasion. King Ferdinand I again resident in Palermo.

1810 - Ferdinand II born in Palermo.

1812 - Under British influence, feudalism is abolished by new Constitution.

1814 - General restoration of Jesuits in Europe (rehabilitated in southern Italy 1804).

1814-1815 - Congress of Vienna.

1815 - Joachim Murat executed in Calabria following attempted incursion.

1816 - Kingdom of the Two Sicilies is established following Ferdinand's return to Naples; Sicilian constitution is suppressed when Neapolitan and Sicilian crowns are formally unified for the first time since 1282.

1818 - The *Ferdinando I* becomes the first steamship in the Mediterranean.

1820 - Civil marriages and vital statistics records instituted in Sicily.

1821 - Rothschild Bank opens in Naples (closes in 1863 following unification).

1825 - Ferdinand I dies, Francis I becomes king.

1829 - Order of Francis I founded to reward merit in the arts and sciences.

1830 - Francis I dies, Ferdinand II crowned.

1832 - First glass recycling program introduced in Two Sicilies. First steel suspension bridge in Italy constructed over Gagliano River.

1836 - Maria Cristina of Savoy, queen consort, dies; beatified in 2014.

1839 - First railroad in Italy built from Naples to Portici. First gas-fuelled public lighting system introduced in Two Sicilies.

1841 - First seismic observatory in the world established at Mount Vesuvius.

1846 - First commercial electric telegraphs introduced in Europe.

1846-1848 - Bad grain harvests in Sicily and across Europe; Potato Famine worsens in Ireland.

1847 - Revolts in Messina. *Giglio delle Onde* becomes first steamship with screw propulsion in the Mediterranean.

1848 - Revolts begin in Palermo and spread across Europe. New constitution is enacted but soon abolished.

1852 - Two Sicilies sets up first functioning electric telegraph in Italy.

1856 - Britain and France recall their ambassadors from Naples. Congress of Paris formally ends Crimean War.

1859 - Ferdinand II dies, Francis II becomes King of the Two Sicilies.

1860 - Northern Italian troops led by Giuseppe Garibaldi (1807-1882) embark in Sicily. At Bronte, Nino Bixio's troops become the first military contingent identified with the united Italy to summarily execute civilians. Sicily is annexed to the Kingdom of Italy.

Kingdom of Italy

1861 - King Francis II of the Two Sicilies surrenders Gaeta north of Naples, exiled. Victor Emmanuel II of Savoy, King of Sardinia, becomes King of Italy.

1862 - Fenestrelle, a "secret" Alpine prison for political detainees (mostly Two-Sicilies loyalists), becomes Italy's first concentration camp.

1866 - Revolt against Piedmontese occupation and annexation in Palermo; protests suppressed by Piedmontese troops.

1867 - Ecclesiastical property confiscated in Sicily, leading to closure of most monastic schools and (in the absence of state schools to substitute these) decrease in general literacy.

1877 - Mandatory public education instituted but few public (state) schools established south of Rome before 1900.

1882 - First major sulfur mines (rather than open pits) excavated in Sicily, resulting in exploitation of child labor.

1887 - Francesco Crispi (1818-1901), a bigamist, becomes Italy's first Sicilian prime minister (1887-1891 and 1893-1896).

1894 - *Fasci Siciliani,* a rural labor movement founded in Sicily, suppressed by force and summary trials. Death of King Francis II of the Two Sicilies in exile.

1896 - Italians suffer major defeat by Ethiopians at Battle of Adwa; some 7,000 Italian troops killed and 3,000 taken prisoner. Italy earns disdain of world's great military powers (Russia openly supports Ethiopia politically). Crispi government falls following resulting protests in Rome.

1897 - Italy, followed by France and Britain, recognizes Ethiopia.

1898 - Bava-Beccaris Massacre in Milan; prompts fall of Di Rudinì government.

1900 - King Umberto I assassinated at Monza in reprisal for massacre of 1898.

1908 - Earthquake and tsunami destroy most of Messina, killing as many as 100,000 in Sicily and Calabria; government's response is woefully inadequate.

1911 - National census data reports that some 58 percent of Sicilians are illiterate. Italy occupies Libya (formerly an Ottoman territory), and many Sicilians migrate to the new Italian colony despite civil unrest. Rhodes is also occupied.

1915 - Italy enters the First World War.

1920 - Italy formally annexes occupied South Tyrol by terms of treaty ending First World War.

1922 - Fascist government installed by King Victor Emmanuel III; becomes dictatorship by 1924. Rijeka and territories in Istrian peninsula, now Slovenia and Croatia, occupied (illegally) by Italy, annexed formally in 1924. Fascists institute program to populate this region and South Tyrol (see above) with Italian-speaking settlers; by 1940 Italian is the principal spoken language of Bozen (Bolzano) and remains so today.

1924 - Giacomo Matteotti, member of parliament and outspoken opponent of Fascism, kidnapped and murdered by Fascist secret police; murderers granted amnesty by King Victor Emmanuel III.

1925 - Death of Maria Sophia, last Queen of the Two Sicilies, in exile.

1925-1929 - Cesare Mori (1871-1942), the "Iron Prefect," nearly eradicates the Mafia, but in 1943 the Americans will vacate convictions of those posing as anti-Fascists, appointing several as mayors of small towns.

1929 - Lateran Treaties establish diplomatic relations between Italy and Vatican, ending state of war that lasted almost 60 years. Ecclesiastical marriages celebrated in Sicily since 1861 are thereby retroactively recognized by the Italian state, where Catholicism is confirmed as state religion.

1930 - *Enciclopedia Italiana* cites Antonio Meucci as inventor of the telephone.

1936 - Italy invades Ethiopia and initiates genocide by poison gas and other means; is condemned by League of Nations. Sicilians and other Italians settle in "Italian West Africa" as part of rural colonization program. Under terms of Paris Peace Treaty of 1947, Italy will lose colonies and pay Ethiopia US $25 million in reparations, principally "in kind" (construction projects).

1937 - Physicist Emilio Segré discovers first "artificial" element, Technetium (Tc), at University of Palermo. Italy resigns from League of Nations.

1938 - Racial laws against Jews in Italy restrict civil rights, holding of public positions (including professorships), marriages with Gentiles. Emilio Segré, who is Jewish, leaves Italy; working with other scientists at the University of California at Berkeley (where he is later appointed professor), he discovers Astatine and Plutonium-239, and receives Nobel Prize in 1959.

1939 - Italy invades and occupies Albania; by terms of Paris Peace Treaty of 1947 Italy will pay Albania US $5 million in reparations.

1940 - Italy declares war on France and Great Britain. Italy invades Greece but its offensive is repulsed by counterattacks in Greece and Albania (the first Allied land victory of the Second World War). Under Paris Peace Treaty of 1947, Italy will pay Greece US $105 million in reparations.

1941 - Italians defeated by British and Ethiopian forces in Ethiopia; Italy declares war on the United States. Germany sends troops into Greece to bolster Italians.

1942-1943 - Allied forces defeat Axis troops in Libya and Tunisia; Italy's ephemeral colonial empire is thus completely dismembered. Italian and German troops are defeated at Stalingrad; under Paris Peace Treaty of 1947, Italy will pay Russia (Soviet Union) US $100 million in reparations.

1943 - Allied carpet bombing of Palermo begins in February; some 98 civilians are killed on first day while historic Magione church sustains extensive damage. In July, Allies occupy Sicily following largest amphibious invasion ever attempted (soon superseded by D-day landings in Normandy); Italian forces under Alfredo Guzzoni flee across Strait of Messina. In response to crushing defeat and loss of Sicily, King Victor Emmanuel III removes Benito Mussolini from power. In September, Italy changes alliance and the king abandons Rome for Brindisi.

1944-1946 - Reclaiming the Istria region annexed to Italy in 1924, Slovenian and Croatian partisans expel or kill numerous Italians, relocated there under Fascist policy, in "Foibe" incidents. Allies and United Nations regard such reprisals, ubiquitous during the war, as reaction to earlier Axis actions, but with Paris Peace Treaty (see below) Allied troops occupy free territory of Trieste in 1947.

1945 - War ends in Italy in late April, when Benito Mussolini is killed by Italian partisans armed by Americans. Allies acknowledge this resistance movement as cooperative but undisciplined; partisans sometimes undertook reprisals on unarmed civilians and had agreed to consign Fascist hierarchs to Allies. Women granted the right to vote.

Italian Republic

1946 - In May, Sicily granted political semi-autonomy by King Umberto II on American orders. In June, Italian women vote for the first time in the popular referendum establishing the Italian Republic. King Umberto II and his young son are exiled while formerly-exiled Bourbon descendants (whose ancestors ruled Sicily until 1860) are permitted free entry into Italy.

1947 - Italy becomes first nation to acknowledge committing *crimes against humanity* (with reference to genocide in Ethiopia); generic war crimes also acknowledged and Italy begins payment of reparations to Ethiopia, Greece, other countries (total of US $360 million). Paris Peace Treaty (10 February) formally restores Rijeka and territories in Istrian peninsula (in Slovenia and Croatia) to Yugoslavia; Italy legally divested of *all* colonial possessions (Somalia, Libya, Rhodes). Allied troops leave Italy except for Trieste. Portella della Ginestra massacre results in deaths of 11 protesters near Piana degli Albanesi.

1948 - Italy begins receiving funds from the Marshall Plan even as it pays reparations to Russia (Soviet Union) and other nations; American aid to Italy totals $1.2 billion by 1952. Constitution of the Italian Republic chartered; semi-autonomy guaranteed to Sicily, Aosta, South Tyrol.

1949 - Land reforms fragment large agricultural estates (latifondi) in Sicily and permit distribution of property. Italian immigration to the United States resumes.

1950 - Salvatore Giuliano, bandit and outspoken proponent of Sicilian independence movement, is killed.

1952 - Danilo Dolci (1924-1997) establishes social movement at Partinico to combat economic inequality and organized crime.

1953 - Petroleum discovered off Sicily's southeastern coasts.

1954 - Allied Military Government cedes control of Trieste to Italy and Yugoslavia.

1955 - Italy permitted entry into United Nations; last Italian prisoners of war repatriated from Soviet Union (Russia).

1957 - Treaty of Rome establishes framework for European Union. Sicilian Mafia "Cupola" meeting in Palermo and American Mafia "Commission" meeting in Apalachin (New York).

1958 - *The Leopard* by Giuseppe Tomasi di Lampedusa (1896-1957) is published; in translation it is the first Sicilian work to become an international bestseller. The novel impugns "official" views of the *Risorgimento*.

1959 - United States naval air base established at Sigonella near Catania; a NATO base is later constructed next to this site.

1962 - Film *Divorce Italian Style,* with its story set in Sicily, is released abroad, bringing censorious attention to Italy's lack of divorce statutes.

1964 - Cardinal Ernesto Ruffini (1888-1967), Archbishop of Palermo, refutes existence of the Mafia and implies that social worker Danilo Dolci and author Giuseppe Tomasi di Lampedusa have "defamed" Sicily.

1968 - Towns in Belice Valley destroyed by major earthquake receive little emergency relief; most reconstruction funds are misappropriated.

1970 - Italian parliament legalizes divorce; law is confirmed by referendum in 1974.

1978 - Italy legalizes abortion.

1981 - Italy bans theatrical release of *The Lion of the Desert,* a motion picture depicting civilian massacres in Italian-occupied Libya; national censorship ends with broadcast on Italian satellite television on 11 June 2009.

1982 - Mafia assassinates Carlo Alberto Dalla Chiesa, Prefect of Palermo; organized crime is recognized in law as a felony.

1983 - Death of Umberto II, exiled King of Italy.

1984 - With update of Vatican concordat of 1929 (Lateran Treaties), Roman Catholicism ceases to be the official religion of Italy but Catholic Church continues to be recognized as a "state within a state." Francis II of the Two Sicilies interred in Naples.

1987 - Mafiosi sentenced in "Maxiprocesso," first major trial of Sicilian organized crime figures in Italy under new laws, coinciding with "Pizza Connection" trial in the United States.

1992 - Judges Falcone and Borsellino assassinated by the Mafia.

1993 - Giuseppe Puglisi, a Catholic priest, is murdered by the Mafia in Palermo's Brancaccio district. Beatified in 2013.

1996 - Italian legislation makes rape a violent felony comparable to assault rather than a minor (and rarely-punished) "offense against public decency" but convictions remain a rarity.

1997 - Italy fully implements last remaining conditions making it part of the Schengen Area.

2000 - In view of impending introduction of the euro, Italy mints the last *lira,* the currency introduced nationwide with unification.

2009 - Stalking becomes a felony crime in Italy but high burden of proof makes convictions rare.

2012 - Italy abolishes legal distinction between children born to wed and unwed parents; in this year 25 percent of births in Italy nationally are to unwed couples, around 18 percent in Sicily.

2014 - Various legal restrictions on the use of reproductive technologies in fertility treatment (gamete donation, in vitro fertilization, etc.) lifted in Italy.

2017 - Parliament refuses to pass law based on *ius soli* principle that would make children born in Italy citizens regardless of parentage.

APPENDIX 2

Milestones 1735-1860

The territory of the former Two Sicilies *circa* 1862 had a population of some eight million, with 3,216 students enrolled in its public universities, almost half the Italian national total (excluding the city of Rome) of 7,957. Piedmont-Sardinia, with a population of slightly over four million, had far fewer university students *per capita*.

An interesting list of "firsts," to which your authors have added, was presented in Michele Vocino's *Primati del Regno di Napoli* (1950).

Herewith, posthumous plaudits to a forgotten country in the form of a list of noteworthy achievements in the Kingdom of the Two Sicilies relative to the other pre-unitary Italian states.

- First pension system in Italy (2 percent deduction from salaries),
- Most printing presses of any Italian city (Naples with 113),
- Lowest commercial and personal taxes in Italy,
- Largest international commercial bank in Italy (de Rothschild in Naples),
- Largest naval yards based on number of employees (1900 in Castellammare di Stabia),
- Largest iron and steel engineering-manufacturing plant in Italy (at Pietrarsa),
- Largest iron casting foundry in Italy (Ferdinandea in Calabria),
- Oldest continuously-active opera house in Europe, the San Carlo in Naples (1737, rebuilt in 1816),

- Largest porcelain factory in Italy (Capodimonte, 1743),
- Largest royal residence in Italy (Caserta, 1752),
- First university chair/department in economics (Antonio Genovesi, Naples, 1754),
- First *public* botanical gardens in Italy (opened in Palermo in 1795); others were private or scholastic,
- First Italian state to recognize United States (1796),
- Dwarf planet Ceres first observed (Giuseppe Piazzi, Palermo, 1801),
- First modern paved carriageway in Italy (Piana-Palermo, 1810),
- First steamship in the Mediterranean, the Ferdinando I (1818),
- First glass recycling program (1832),
- First steel suspension bridge in Italy (Gagliano River in 1832, components from Mongiana Works),
- First gas-fuelled public lighting system (1839),
- First railroad in Italy (Naples-Portici, 1839),
- First seismic observatory in the world (Vesuvius 1841),
- First steamboat with screw propulsion in the Mediterranean (the Giglio delle Onde 1847),
- First functioning electric telegraph in Italy (1852),
- Ranked 3rd country in the world for industrial development (1st in Italy) by Paris International Exhibition (1856),
- First adhesive postage stamps in Italy (1857),
- First submarine telegraph in Europe,
- First military steamship in Italy (the Ercole),
- First maritime code in Italy,
- First public housing complex/estate in Italy, 1778 (San Leucio near Caserta),
- Highest per capita number of physicians in Italy (1850-1860),
- First *public* school for the deaf in Italy (Naples, 1788); school founded in Rome in 1784 was private,
- Lowest infant mortality rate in Italy (1850-1860).

INDEX

These entries do not include every significant topic mentioned in this book (for example in Chapter 3 and the Timeline). This index is intended merely as a list of some topics frequently considered in the field of Sicilian Studies.